# THE BIBLE IN 52 WEEKS
# DEVOTIONAL FOR BOYS

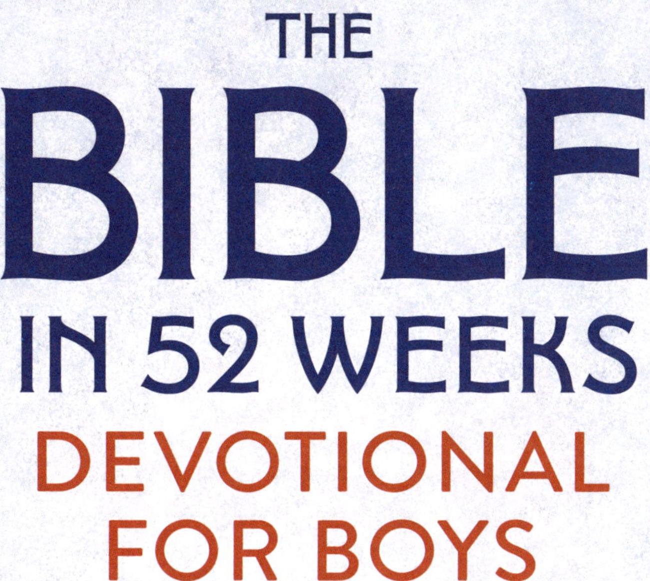

# THE BIBLE IN 52 WEEKS DEVOTIONAL FOR BOYS

## A YEAR OF GROWING IN FAITH

LORD BADU

callisto publishing
an imprint of Sourcebooks

Series Designer: Liz Cosgrove
Art Directors: Richard Tapp, Lisa Schreiber
Art Producers: Samantha Ulban, Stacey Stambaugh
Editors: Jed Bickman, Pamela Bobowicz
Production Editors: Ruth Sakata Corley, Rachel Taenzler
Production Designer: Martin Worthington



Published by Callisto Publishing LLC C/O Sourcebooks LLC
P.O. Box 4410, Naperville, Illinois 60567-4410
(630) 961-3900
callistopublishing.com

Originally published as *52-Week Devotional for Boys* in 2021 in the United States of America by Callisto Kids, an imprint of Callisto Publishing LLC.

Library of Congress Cataloging-in-Publication Data is on file with the publisher.

This product conforms to all applicable CPSC and CPSIA standards.

Source of Production: 1010 Printing Asia Limited, Kwun Tong, Hong Kong, China
Date of Production: July 2025
Run Number: 5050624

Printed and bound in China.
OGP 10 9 8 7 6 5 4 3 2 1

*This book is dedicated to my enthusiastic daughter, Eden-Monroe Badu, and superstar son, Lord Badu, Jr. You both are a blessing from God to me and your mother. We love you!*

# INTRODUCTION

## *Hey, guys!*

My name's Lord Badu, and I'm a husband, father, Bible teacher, and Christian rapper. I've always been passionate about coaching sports like basketball or soccer, but one thing I love about working with God's word is being able to coach in a different way.

My passion is to help young men like you become all that God has created you to be. Let's say I'm your coach, and the playbook is the Bible—it's my job to coach you on how to properly make the plays to win the game of life. I know school can be tough and difficult when you're a young boy. But as you grow up and continue to build your confidence in God, the goal is for you to be unstoppable—just like LeBron James when he goes for a dunk, or Sidney Crosby when he's on the ice.

When you join a sports team, sometimes the coach makes you do hard exercises and drills you don't like, but that's what prepares you for the real game, right? So in this devotional, you're going to deal with anxiety, teamwork, anger, attitude, faith, and many other things. The idea is to read each devotion and reflect on it throughout the week, and then return to it during the year to keep your relationship to the Spirit strong. So don't just read this devotional once. Read it over and over again until it's like a favorite song that's stuck in your head. Remember that these pages aren't just random words and prayers—they'll connect you to God and make you like his son Jesus.

Now I just have one question for you: Are you ready to become unstoppable?

God has your back, so you can never lose!

# A HELPFUL HINT ABOUT BIBLE QUOTATIONS

You don't need to carry your Bible with you to use this devotional because there are scriptures for each week. But if you do want to keep your Bible handy to highlight certain things, I highly recommend it.

If you don't have a traditional Bible, you can download the **YouVersion Bible App** and even listen to the quotation of the day, as well as highlight it on your phone.

There are many Bible versions, or translations. The Bible was written thousands of years ago but was not written in English, so translators took it from the original Hebrew and Greek and translated it into our context and our language. The King James Version (KJV) was first published more than five centuries ago. This is one of the most commonly used versions today. It uses very traditional language.

I think the best version for you would be the New International Version (NIV) because it translates God's word into language that anyone can read and understand.

Here is the difference between the two: While the KJV Bible would say "thou" and "thee," the NIV version says "you" instead of those words. Another example is "thou art"—what do you think that means? If you said "you are," you're right.

# YOU ARE CREATED FOR A SPECIAL PURPOSE ON THIS EARTH

Have your parents ever asked you to do something you were completely terrified to do? Like when you moved to a new school, and they told you to go introduce yourself to the class? The prophet Jeremiah found himself in a similar situation when God told him to go out and speak His word to the people in his community. Jeremiah argued with God and told him, "I can't do it—I'm too young! I don't even know how to speak properly!" But God told him something very important that helped him understand his reason for being on this earth. God said that, before Jeremiah was even in his mother's stomach, he chose him for this special job because he was a special kid. God believed in Jeremiah to accomplish his mission on earth as His prophet.

Whenever you see something like this in the Bible, God is always trying to teach you a lesson. The same way God chose Jeremiah for a special job before he was born, God also created you for a special purpose on this earth. So the more you talk to God, the more He shows you your purpose. And though sometimes you might feel like you can't do the job, God will give you extra strength, which is the Holy Spirit, and help you do it in the best way possible.

*Before I formed you in the womb I knew you, before you were born I set you apart; I appointed you as a prophet to the nations.*

**Jeremiah 1:5**

## Reflect

*Purpose and passion always go together. What are things that you are passionate about that you can use to serve God in school, church, or your community?*

## Respond

*Write a list of seven things that you are great at and passionate about. Come back to it at the end of the week and see what else you can add.*

| TALENTS | THINGS I LOVE TO DO |
|---|---|
| | |
| | |
| | |
| | |
| | |
| | |
| | |

God, thank you for showing me that I have a special purpose. Help me find it and live the way you want me to. Amen.

# DO I GO LEFT, OR DO I GO RIGHT?

It's so easy to follow the crowd because nobody ever wants to be left behind. We all want to fit in with the most "popular" people, because being accepted by them means we'll be accepted by everybody else—and that's a great feeling. I remember in the 5th grade we had a talent show, and I signed up to perform my secret talent: rapping. After I finished rapping and we went out for recess, all the girls in my grade started chasing me and my friends for autographs and pictures, treating us like celebrities. So I know the feeling of wanting to be one of the cool kids.

But later on, the boys who were considered cool started causing trouble in the school. They started talking back to teachers, bullying other students, and doing a bunch of other terrible things.

Jesus says that the way to darkness is a very wide and easy road—and that's the road that most people take because they see most people they know also taking that path. But Jesus also says that while the road to success and doing the right thing is very narrow and difficult, it's the right road to follow.

> *Enter through the narrow gate. For wide is the gate and broad and easy to travel is the path that leads the way to destruction and eternal loss, and there are many who enter through it. But small is the gate and narrow and difficult to travel is the path that leads the way to [everlasting] life, and there are few who find it.*
>
> **Matthew 7:13–14**

## Reflect

*My mom always used to ask me this: If I saw all my friends crossing a road that was unsafe, would I do it too? Or would I choose to wait till there was a safe opportunity?*

## Respond

*Next time you see other kids doing the wrong thing, you don't have to follow them. In fact, do the opposite, because actions speak louder than words. Be a leader by making the right choices and taking the harder path.*

List a few actions on the lines below that you think a good leader would take.

______________________________________________

______________________________________________

______________________________________________

______________________________________________

______________________________________________

> Thank you Lord for showing me that I have the strength and courage to be a leader. Help me always make the right choices that bring me closer to you. Amen.

# TEAMWORK MAKES THE DREAM WORK

Everybody needs a little help sometimes because no one on this earth is perfect. The only person who was ever perfect was Jesus Christ—and he still had 12 friends who helped him in his ministry, because teamwork makes the dream work!

When you look at Exodus 4:10–17, you see that God gave Moses an assignment to talk to the king of Egypt and convince him to set the Israelites free. It was kind of like doing a class presentation—God did the research and all the other hard work, but he asked Moses to give the speech to the class. But Moses started arguing with God, saying that he wasn't qualified to talk in front of the king because he couldn't speak well and stuttered too much. He was scared nobody would understand him and that everyone would laugh. God told Moses not to worry because He would be right beside him, but Moses insisted that he was the wrong guy for the job. Then God remembered that Moses had a brother named Aaron who was good at public speaking. So the two brothers teamed up for the presentation and Moses whispered the words to Aaron, who spoke them to the king.

In the Bible, Moses is considered to be one of the greatest and most powerful prophets ever, yet he was scared to talk in front of people. No matter how strong you may appear to be, there's always something you can't do on your own. It might be a school presentation, or cleaning your basement, or working on your basketball defense. Don't neglect the power of teamwork—it changes everything.

*But Moses said, "Pardon your servant, Lord. Please send someone else." Then the Lord's anger burned against Moses and he said, "What about your brother, Aaron the Levite? I know he can speak well. He is already on his way to meet you, and he will be glad to see you."*

**Exodus 4:13–14**

## Reflect

*The next time you have a chance to be part of a team, jump on it. When you practice teamwork, you open your heart more toward God.*

## Respond

*Make a list of five loved ones you know who would be great teammates. Then write two positive qualities of each of them, like "helps others" or "asks questions." Think about how exactly they help you be successful. Are there ways you help them too?*

Thank you, Father, for allowing me to see the importance of teamwork. Amen.

# YOU CAN CHANGE

When I was growing up, I was known as the troublemaker in my family, church, and school. Teachers would always tell other students to be careful around me because I might lead them into trouble. The funny thing is, I thought I was a great kid, but the reality was that I didn't listen to instructions. I didn't finish my homework on time because I was always watching television. My mom had to ask me a million times to do my chores. And in church, I was always running around in Sunday school leading other kids to do what I was doing. Looking back now, my behavior was terrible. But thank God for grace!

My story is nowhere close to Apostle Paul's, but it is definitely relatable. After Paul's conversion, throughout his life he wrote about 13 letters in the New Testament. The interesting thing is that Paul used to hate Christians so badly that he would send soldiers to kill them. But one day Paul encountered Jesus Christ while he was traveling to Damascus, and from that day, everything changed. One encounter with Jesus can completely change you. No matter what you've done, or the hurtful things you might have said, Jesus is willing to meet you where you are and change you to make you like himself.

*As he neared Damascus on his journey,
suddenly a light from heaven flashed around him.
He fell to the ground and heard a voice say to him,
"Saul, Saul, why do you persecute me?"*

*"Who are you, Lord?" Saul asked.*

*"I am Jesus, whom you are persecuting," he replied.
"Now get up and go into the city, and you will be told
what you must do."*

**Acts 9:3–6**

## Reflect

*One encounter with Jesus is all it takes to transform you from who you are now into who you are supposed to be.*

## Respond

*On the next page, write down your typical daily schedule. Challenge yourself to dedicate two time slots a day to praying and reading God's word so that you can encounter Him. Maybe it's every morning and evening after you've brushed your teeth, or for 15 minutes before breakfast and dinner. Just make sure it's a time when you can sit down and commit to reflecting quietly with God.*

CONTINUED ON NEXT PAGE ➡

CONTINUED FROM PREVIOUS PAGE

| DAILY SCHEDULE | WHEN CAN I PRAY? |
| --- | --- |
| 7 a.m. | |
| 8 a.m. | |
| 9 a.m. | |
| 10 a.m. | |
| 11 a.m. | |
| 12 p.m. | |
| 1 p.m. | |
| 2 p.m. | |
| 3 p.m. | |
| 4 p.m. | |
| 5 p.m. | |
| 6 p.m. | |
| 7 p.m. | |
| 8 p.m. | |

God, I'm asking you this year to help me encounter you in a special way so that my life can be transformed for the better. Amen.

# DON'T LET FEAR GET TO YOU!

Remember when I said it was my goal to make you unstoppable? Do you know why? Because it's fear's goal to make you stoppable. Fear makes you not want to do things, even though you may be good at them. Fear stops you from reaching your highest potential because it knows all the great ways God will use you to change the world for the better.

But while fear thinks it has it all figured out, God let us in on a secret: The Bible says that fear is a spirit, but it has no power over us because God has given us power to overcome it.

Now, there's a big difference between normal fear and spiritual fear. Normal fear is being afraid of things like the dark or leaping from great heights. Spiritual fear is being afraid of standing up for what's right, or meeting new people, or even sharing your testimony. It's anything that we think will cause people to hate us or be against us.

But you can't let that kind of fear rule your life. You are a warrior and can fight with the armor of God to defeat this spirit. All you have to do is always be on guard and deal with it when it tries to come your way. This Bible passage is to show that the spirit of fear is not God's intention for us—that's why He's given us power, love, and self-discipline to defeat it.

*For the Spirit God gave us does not make us timid, but gives us power, love and self-discipline.*

**2 Timothy 1:7**

## Reflect

*Whenever you find yourself in a fearful situation, tell yourself that you have the spirit of power, love, and self-discipline, so you can't lose!*

## Respond

*Write the following three words repeatedly all over the space below.*

**POWER LOVE SELF-DISCIPLINE**

*Try using different colored pens or writing in crazy letters. The more you put your creativity into this activity, the easier you'll find it to feel unafraid. Every morning during the next week, look at this page as a reminder that you have everything you need to conquer your spiritual fear throughout the day.*

Thank you, Lord, that I carry the spirit of power, love, and self-discipline. I know because of you I have nothing to fear. You are an awesome God. Amen.

# ATTITUDE IS EVERYTHING

When you're playing a game, did you know that it's your attitude that determines whether you win or you lose? The mentality you carry in specific situations is everything. For example, let's look at the legendary story of David and Goliath, which can be compared to a football game. The two teams on the field were the Israelites and the Philistines. The Philistines had a star player named Goliath from Gath. Goliath was 9 feet and 5 inches tall and wore 91 pounds of equipment. Imagine how big this guy must've looked. The Israelites were afraid to take him on even though they had so many good players—and God—on their side. Sure, it must have been scary to see him in his armor, but they were still a strong team who could fight. And yet they all backed down because, in their minds, they were already defeated.

The hero of this story is a boy named David who stayed home at first to take care of his dad's sheep. But because David knew that his brother was on the battlefield and probably hungry and tired, he decided to go deliver food to him. When David arrived, he saw the Israelite army of the Lord cowering in the presence of their opponent.

Unafraid, David looked at Goliath and asked, "Who is that guy resisting the Lord's Army?"

David came with a winning mentality. He knew as soon as he saw this giant that he would win the battle because he knew the source of his strength: God. In fact, he was so confident that he asked what the reward was for taking down the giant.

Then David said one sentence that ultimately showed that the battle was over. Are you ready for it? "You come against me with sword, spear, and javelin," he said. "But I come against you in the name of the Lord of Armies, the God of the ranks of Israel." David understood that while he wasn't a physical match for Goliath, with God on his side, he could defeat the giant in his own way.

The mind is a very powerful thing that can make you or break you. You need to develop a winning mentality no matter what situation you find yourself in, because God always has your back.

*This day the Lord will deliver you into my hands.*

**1 Samuel 17:46**

## Reflect

*A winning mindset will help you become the best person to be around because people will always be encouraged when they hear you speak.*

## Respond

*Search the Bible for seven quotes with uplifting messages that inspire you and write them down in the chart on the next page. Can you memorize one every day of this week?*

| WHAT IS THE QUOTE? | WHO SAID IT? | IN WHAT BOOK WAS IT SAID? |
| --- | --- | --- |
| **Day 1** | | |
| **Day 2** | | |
| **Day 3** | | |
| **Day 4** | | |
| **Day 5** | | |
| **Day 6** | | |
| **Day 7** | | |

Thank you, God, for giving me strength to defeat any giant in my life. Help me always trust in you. Amen.

# BE A GOOD EXAMPLE

It's God's intention for you to be a leader. One day you will lead a family, a workplace, a church, a team, or something even bigger. When you're a leader, everyone watches everything that you do and say—the good and the bad. Have you noticed that when you're in school and you do something cool, people often try to do the same thing? Because you're a leader at heart. Jesus was your ultimate leader. He was perfect without any wrongs and showed you what it means to be perfect because he knew that you can't fully be that way. But the one thing you can do is try your hardest to be like Christ and lead others to be like him.

That was what Paul was talking about when he told the church at Corinth to follow his example. We all know Paul was definitely not perfect. But after his first encounter with Jesus changed him completely, Paul was so happy that he wanted to be just like him. So, as he continued to grow spiritually, he told others to follow him as he tried to follow Christ.

This is a worthy goal to have as a young man. Be a great example for people around you, and let them follow your actions as you follow Christ and make his name great. I always say it's an honor to be chosen by God to be a leader in His kingdom.

*Follow my example, as I follow the example of Christ.*

**1 Corinthians 11:1**

## Reflect

*They say every great leader was once a great follower. In order for people to follow you, you must follow somebody—and that somebody is Jesus.*

## Respond

*I want you to look for someone you would want to be like when you get older. Ask to interview them so you can learn more about the way they live. Let this person be a good man—it can be someone from your school or church, your coach, or even a sibling. When you interview them, ask them the following five questions and then come up with two more of your own. Once you have their answers, choose one to reflect on each day for a week and think about how you can apply that wisdom to your own life.*

1. In what ways do you try to be a good man following Christ's example?
2. What do you do when you face spiritual fear, and how do you overcome it?
3. What was the biggest lesson you learned in school about being a good man?
4. What are the most important qualities of being a leader?

CONTINUED ON NEXT PAGE ➡

CONTINUED FROM PREVIOUS PAGE

5. What was a time in your life when you faced the challenges that come with being a leader and a good man?

6. ______________________________

______________________________

______________________________

______________________________

7. ______________________________

______________________________

______________________________

______________________________

Lord, help me be a great leader in my generation. Help me lead more people to you as they follow the example that I show. Amen.

# HAVE FRIENDS WHO STAND BY YOU

It can be hard to find truly good friends because a lot of people only seem to care about themselves. In the 4th grade, I remember I left class to go to the washroom, and I saw kids throwing tissue on the ceiling. I walked in and laughed a bit at what was going on, then left to go back to class. When the janitor came to clean the washroom, he saw the mess that the students made and everyone who was there got detention. One of the kids told the teachers that I was also there, even though I hadn't done anything wrong. But because that kid lied about me, I got detention for something I didn't do.

That event really woke me up and taught me that real friends don't get you into trouble. But when trouble happens, you want people who will stand with you through thick and thin—like Shadrach, Meshach, and Abednego.

In the book of Daniel, Shadrach, Meshach, and Abednego stood up to King Nebuchadnezzar II when he told them to bow down to a golden image of himself. Because these boys were Hebrew, they understood who their God was and knew the commandment of not worshiping any other idol. Even when the king threatened them and threw them into a fire, they all stood together because they were friends who had each other's back.

We all need friends like Shadrach, Meshach, and Abednego because we all have times when we truly need somebody. Maybe your friends helped you stand up to a bully at school, or sat with you at lunch when you were alone, or played with you more at recess. I had three best friends in my life, and I met them all at church. We had a common interest—God—so I knew what they stood for, and they knew what I stood for. After 20 years, we're still best friends because our values have never changed.

The best thing about this story of Shadrach, Meshach, and Abednego is that, because all these friends stood together to defend their faith in God, an angel showed up in the fire with them, and, ultimately, God saved them!

> *If we are thrown into the blazing furnace, the God we serve is able to deliver us from it, and he will deliver us from Your Majesty's hand. But even if he does not, we want you to know, Your Majesty, that we will not serve your gods or worship the image of gold you have set up.*
>
> **Daniel 3:17–18**

## Reflect

*Try to always to be the best friend possible to somebody in the same way God is your best friend. That way you'll be able to show the love of God through the way you live and draw others to the kingdom.*

## Respond

*Every evening this week before you go to sleep, think of a different person in your life who you value as a great friend. Write their name and why you appreciate them. Then find time to share your thoughts with them so that they can feel uplifted and supported by your loyal friendship.*

God, thank you for all the good friends I have. I pray you continue to help me meet good friends and build trustworthy relationships as I grow older. Amen.

# FIND HAPPINESS IN GIVING TO OTHERS

A few weeks ago, I was reading an article that said half of the people in the world live on less than five dollars a day. Think about this when your parents give you money to buy lunch at school or get a tasty treat for yourself. That one meal for you could be worth the same as two days of food for someone else. Imagine having to make your food last that long.

Apostle Paul understood both the life of having very little and the life of abundance. But when given a choice between the two, he said that he'd much rather give than receive. As a missionary, he could have chosen to receive money from the church, but he decided to work hard at being a tent maker so that he didn't need to burden anyone by asking them for money. There weren't many wealthy people around at that time, and he didn't want to ask anyone to give more than they had. Paul understood when Jesus said, "It is better to give than to receive," and he really lived by those words. He understood that he didn't need much to live and so he'd rather give to somebody else and see the smile on their face.

The interesting thing about giving is that it somehow always comes back to you because God knows He can trust you, and He sees that you aren't greedy. Because many of your friends have things like video games, cell phones, or computers, it's easy to think it's essential for you to have them too. But these aren't mandatory things you need—they're just great things to have. God's message to you today is to learn how to be selfless with the things He allows you to have. Because you are trying to be like Christ, you should also be as generous as he is. You don't always have to give away everything—just the extra stuff you could do without.

> *In everything I did, I showed you that by this kind of hard work we must help the weak, remembering the words the Lord Jesus himself said: "It is more blessed to give than to receive."*
>
> **Acts 20:35**

## Reflect

*When you become a giver, you become like Christ. The best gift he gave was his life for you, so every time you give from your heart, you are reflecting Jesus in your life. Last Christmas, my mother and I sent clothes to people who were less fortunate. When I saw photos of how happy those people were when they received their items, it was so rewarding. There will never be a greater feeling than I had that day. It's truly a bigger blessing to give than to receive.*

## Respond

*How many toys, books, or clothes do you have that you don't need anymore? Put a box in your room and each day this week, add one item you own that you could give to someone else. Or if you already know what you can give away, make a list below. At the end of the week, pack them up and find a way to give*

CONTINUED ON NEXT PAGE ➡

CONTINUED FROM PREVIOUS PAGE

*them to somebody who needs them more. You're going to feel extremely good after you see the joy on their faces.*

I am grateful for all the things that I have. I know a lot of people may not have these things, but I pray that you give me the heart to give and not be sad about it. Amen.

# THE TRUTH WILL SET YOU FREE

When I was young, I found it easy to turn anything into a joke, and I noticed that no matter what I said, people would always laugh. So to entertain everyone, I'd impersonate things people said and did, and I'd sometimes even turn sad moments into funny ones. But as time went by, I started making up stories to sustain my ability to make others laugh, which meant I had to start lying. That made me feel really guilty because I wasn't showing integrity, and I didn't feel like my true self.

In Proverbs 12:22, the Lord says that He dislikes lying lips because they can get innocent people in big trouble. It's important to stay true to your word because the spirit of God lives inside of you. Embrace the mentality that you won't do something that makes God sad and that can potentially hurt others, and that you'll always be a person who tells the truth. Anytime you think about lying to somebody, switch roles for a moment and imagine how you'd feel if someone did that to you.

Have you heard the story of the boy who cried wolf? A young kid kept lying to people in his town, saying a wolf was coming to eat them, and they should run. He did it so many times that they stopped believing him. But when a wolf really did come to their town, everyone ended up getting hurt because they thought he was lying. The moral of the story is to always tell the truth.

*The Lord detests lying lips,*
*but he delights in people who are trustworthy.*

**Proverbs 12:22**

## Reflect

*Think about how dangerous it is to tell a lie for no reason and consider the consequences.*

## Respond

*Sometimes we tell lies without even realizing it, like when we exaggerate while telling a story, or we don't admit to something because we don't want to get into trouble. Throughout this week, try to catch yourself whenever you tell a lie and then take the right action to tell the truth. It might be helpful to write them down here first and then think about how you can be more honest in those circumstances.*

Lord, I am sorry for the things I have done wrong against you or anybody. I repent and ask that you forgive my sins. Help me be holy as you are holy and help me live a life pleasing to you in Jesus's name. Amen.

# LIVE THE GREATEST COMMANDMENTS

Many times when I read the Bible as a kid, I'd get confused and ask myself how I could possibly follow all of it. Have you ever had that overwhelming moment where you want to obey God, but it seems like it's too much? Well, I want to share with you how Jesus changed everything.

We all used to look to the Ten Commandments as the perfect standard to go to heaven. But because God saw that we can't fully follow everything, He sent His son Jesus to come and do it for us to set an example. The beauty of this is that Jesus did everything he could do to bring you back to God.

Many people think that Jesus came to change the law that God gave to Moses, but he didn't—he came to fulfill it. If you look closely at the Ten Commandments, it's in two major categories that are easy to remember. Let me show you.

The first four have to do with loving God with all your heart:

1. You shall have no other gods before me.
2. You shall not make idols.
3. You shall not take the name of the Lord your God in vain.
4. Remember the Sabbath day to keep it holy.

The last six have to do with loving your neighbor:

5. Honor your father and your mother.
6. You shall not murder.
7. You shall not commit adultery.
8. You shall not steal.
9. You shall not bear false witness against your neighbor.
10. You shall not covet.

So Jesus didn't change anything, he just made it clearer to understand, because when you truly understand something that God has said, it's easier to put into action. He wants you to make these commandments a priority in your life.

> *Jesus replied: "'Love the Lord your God with all your heart and with all your soul and with all your mind.' This is the first and greatest commandment."*
>
> **Matthew 22:37–38**

## Reflect

*Loving God and loving people are the greatest commandments you can ever live by. If you follow these two principles, it will change your life and the lives of those around you.*

## Respond

*Write the scripture above on a piece of paper, memorize it, and say it every morning throughout this week. Use the space below to think about how you can put the words into action in your everyday life.*

Thank you, God, for sending your son to do what we could not do. Help me love you and obey you, and love my neighbor as you have commanded. Amen.

# LOOK UNTO JESUS AND BE LIKE HIM

Imagine spending the majority of your time with Jesus like the disciples did when he was physically on earth. How many amazing things do you think you'd experience? Like the time when Jesus wanted to go pray late at night, and he told his disciples to go in the boat ahead of him and meet him on the other side. As they got into the middle of the sea, the wind grew stronger and the boat started rocking violently. The disciples thought they were all going to be thrown into the water.

But then came Jesus walking across the water to save his disciples. When they saw him coming from afar, everyone was scared because he looked like a ghost. Jesus reassured them that it was him and told them not to be afraid. Peter responded, "Jesus, if that's you, tell me to walk on the water and come to you!" So Jesus told him to come, and Peter started walking on the water—but when he looked at the storm around him, he started to sink. Instead of focusing on Jesus, Peter got distracted by the things around him, like the rain and the wind.

When you have a rough day at school, or you're just feeling down in general, try to remember that's not how Jesus wants you to feel. He wants you to focus on him and gain courage, remembering that nothing has power over you and you can defeat any obstacle that comes your way. Keep looking unto Jesus!

*"Come," he said. Then Peter got down out of the boat, walked on the water and came toward Jesus. But when he saw the wind, he was afraid and, beginning to sink, cried out, "Lord, save me!"*

**Matthew 14:29–30**

## Reflect

*Life will be difficult at times, no matter how young or old you are. We all have our problems, but the key lesson that God is trying to show us is to always fix our eyes on Jesus.*

## Respond

*When Peter focused on Jesus, he conquered fear, and he wasn't worried about the things that could make him drown. Write down three things that can happen to you when you start looking to Jesus. Whenever you face a challenge this week, think about these three things and how they can bring you strength.*

Lord, help me always focus on Jesus, no matter the issues I go through in life. Amen.

# BE STRONG AND COURAGEOUS

Have you ever heard the word courageous? It means the ability to do something that frightens you. In other words, it means to be brave. As a young man, God wants you to be strong and courageous because you are the example that a lot of people will look at. A great leader once told me that, whether you try to or not, you'll influence at least 10,000 people in your lifetime. Think about that impact!

Moses was the leader of the Israelites, and right before he got to the promised land, he died. So God decided to install a new leader, Joshua, who was a follower of Moses. Imagine all the pressure Joshua must have felt about taking the lead from Moses. Luckily, God gave him instructions so he wouldn't fail. He told Joshua to be brave and stick to the laws that Moses taught him, and he'd be successful. All Joshua had to do was follow the perfect plan that was already laid out for him.

In this same way, God has given you instructions so that you can be successful in anything you do in life. He just requires you to be strong and courageous because not everyone will agree with you or be willing to help and support you. But if you have mental toughness and can stand and be brave, you'll be all that God has called on you to be.

*Be strong and very courageous. Be careful*
*to obey all the law my servant Moses gave you;*
*do not turn from it to the right or to the left,*
*that you may be successful wherever you go.*

**Joshua 1:7**

## Reflect

*In life, it's natural that you'll experience fear, but if God is telling you to be strong and courageous, it means you have the ability to do it. So, do it!*

## Respond

*Take a piece of paper and write "I am strong and courageous" in big letters. Post it somewhere you walk by all the time, like your bedroom dresser, a mirror, or in a doorway. Each time you see it, repeat it to yourself three times in your head. After one week, come back to this page and write down how you feel differently about yourself now.*

God, thank you for making me strong and courageous. I am able to fight every battle that comes my way. You are an amazing God. Amen.

# NEVER CHEAT

Cheaters never win and winners never cheat. All my teachers and coaches told me this when I was around your age. I always used to think it was wrong because, a lot of the time, someone who cheats does win. But then I realized they only win for that moment.

Let's say you were doing a math test and you got almost all of the answers perfect because you opened your textbook when the teacher wasn't looking. After everyone gets their marks back and they realize you got the highest mark, everyone is going to come to you for help or ask you questions that you may not know the answer to unless you have the textbook. How do you think that's going to make you feel when you don't really know the answers? You're not the winner anymore.

Or say you're representing your school or church in a race. Instead of waiting for the "ready, set, go!" you start running at "ready, set." You might cross the finish line first, but when everyone sees that you cheated in the beginning, they're more likely to give the trophy to the real winner who didn't cheat. The Bible gives you this lesson to illustrate that an athlete's efforts are wasted unless he competes according to the rules. In biblical terms, if you choose to not follow the Bible's guidelines, you won't receive a trophy because you can't disregard God's word and think you can still be a winner.

Remember that God wants you to be honest and fair with one another so you can reflect His love to other people.

*Similarly, anyone who competes as an athlete does not receive the victor's crown except by competing according to the rules.*

**2 Timothy 2:5**

## Reflect

*If you ran a race and you knew you finished first but you officially came second because someone cheated, how would you feel about that? Following the rules is the honest thing to do.*

## Respond

*Each day this week, think of a different rule you have to follow in your life. Write them down here and then, with an adult you trust, talk about how each rule was made to keep you safe.*

1. ______________________
2. ______________________
3. ______________________
4. ______________________
5. ______________________
6. ______________________
7. ______________________

God, please help me follow all the rules that have been set in place for the good of others.

# YOUR FOUR STEPS TO SALVATION

If you've gotten this far in this devotional, you must really want to know more about what Jesus did for us and how that affects our lives. Jesus is the most powerful and amazing person we will ever know. He has the power to raise the dead, open the eyes of the blind, and heal the sick. He is supposed to be a part of our everyday lives and everything we do because he is our Lord.

Many people have heard of Jesus and what he has done, but a lot of people don't really know him personally. The interesting thing is that he wants to have a close friendship with anyone who is willing. What's amazing about this relationship is that the more you talk to Jesus and are with him, the more you start to be like him. He changes everything bad about you and makes it good because He is perfect, and he also wants to make you perfect.

It's very simple to be in a relationship with Jesus. Just remember these four things:

1. **Realize that you're imperfect.** Know you are capable of sinning and cannot be perfect in the eyes of God. By nature, we are like Adam and Eve, and though God says not to do certain things, we often end up doing them.

2. **Realize that sin leads to separation from God.** This means that if you keep deciding to make the wrong decision, you will keep sinning against God. This can make you unworthy of entering heaven because sinning is disobedient to God. You have to remember that God is holy, so we have to be as holy as He is.

3. **Realize Jesus died, was buried, and then resurrected for you.** Jesus had to give his life so that you and I can be forgiven of our sins and go to heaven with him when he comes back. The resurrection represents a life of victory over sin and the evil of this world.
4. **Repent, and accept Jesus.** When you repent, you change your mind and change your life to think and live the way Jesus would think and live. To repent is to stop making the wrong decisions and follow a righteous path that is pleasing to God.

*For God so loved the world that he gave his one and only Son, that whoever believes in him shall not perish but have eternal life.*

**John 3:16**

## Reflect

*Jesus loves you so much that he gave his life so that you can join him in heaven. Wouldn't it be amazing walking on the righteous path to God? The Bible says the angels rejoice when one soul comes to Jesus—in other words, there's a huge party being thrown for you in heaven.*

## Respond

*The great thing about God is that He is forgiving, so even if you've made wrong decisions in the past, you can still work to be better in future. Before you go to sleep each night this week,*

CONTINUED ON NEXT PAGE ➡

CONTINUED FROM PREVIOUS PAGE

*think of a time when you made a wrong decision that might disappoint God. Write down a way you can make a change so that your behavior is more in line with a righteous path. At the end of the week, look at everything you've written and use it as an action plan for living in a way that will please God.*

God, thank you for accepting me into your family. I am renewed because of the precious love of Jesus. Thank you for your loving kindness toward me. Amen.

# DO YOU HAVE THE FRUIT OF THE SPIRIT?

Would you agree that every apple tree grows oranges sometimes? No. Because that's not true. Every apple tree bears apples, and every orange tree bears oranges. This is the same thing for those of us who call ourselves followers of Jesus. We are like a tree that bears specific types of fruits so that people know who we are when they see us. You can never confuse an apple tree for an orange tree because they are different.

For Christians, the Bible lists out fruit—the behaviors and attitudes that we are supposed to demonstrate in our lifestyle so people can know we are true followers of Jesus. Of course, it's going to take some time to develop all of them, but you can build the ones that you know already and then add more of the following:

**Love:** How much love do you have for people? Think about how you treat your parents. If you are respectful of them, you must have a lot of love for them. Is this something you're growing in?

**Joy:** Are you joyful even when things go bad? Apostle Paul would sing hymns and songs of praise when he was in prison to show how joyful he was that God saved him. If he can rejoice in prison, can't we rejoice in times of hardship? That's something you can work on.

**Peace:** Are you a peaceful person, or do you like it when there's trouble? Jesus said blessed are the peacemakers. Try your hardest to be one.

**Patience:** Patience is a virtue. It's one of the best things to have because you will never rush into anything you don't need to.

**Kindness:** It's always great to show kindness to everybody because you are reflecting the character of God. And if you give kindness, the universal law is that you will get it back.

**Goodness:** When you have goodness, you always have the desire to avoid doing anything bad. Goodness is a trait God carries, and His goodness is forevermore.

**Faithfulness:** Make it a goal to be as faithful to God as He is to you. Faithfulness is another word for loyalty. If you can be loyal to a teammate on the field, why not be loyal to the God of the universe who wants to be your friend?

**Gentleness:** Gentleness is the opposite of aggressiveness or rudeness. We are called to be gentle people and also gentle spirited.

**Self-control:** Self-control is the key to success in anything. You want to be able to have control over your thoughts and actions so you don't do or say something you might regret later.

*But the fruit of the Spirit is love, joy, peace, forbearance, kindness, goodness, faithfulness, gentleness and self-control. Against such things there is no law.*

**Galatians 5:22–23**

## Reflect

*Think of the fruit of the spirit as one fruit that contains all these qualities. So even if you don't show them yet, they are all in you, and you just need to work on exercising them more often.*

*By working to embody the fruit of the spirit, you'll be able to live a life that reflects God in his fullness.*

## Respond

*In column 1 of the chart on the next page, write down the qualities you think you need to develop further as a follower of Jesus. In column 2, write down the steps you can take this week to turn these weaknesses into strengths.*

CONTINUED ON NEXT PAGE ➡

CONTINUED FROM PREVIOUS PAGE

| QUALITIES YOU THINK YOU NEED TO DEVELOP FURTHER | STEPS YOU CAN TAKE TO TURN THESE WEAKNESSES INTO STRENGTHS |
|---|---|
| | |
| | |
| | |

God, please help me grow in the fruit of the spirit and help me be more like your son Jesus. Amen.

# LOVE YOUR ENEMIES

We've all experienced that bully or person who we don't necessarily like to be around. They are in schools, community centers, churches, and sometimes even homes. When I was a kid, there was a boy in my neighborhood who would always chase me when he saw me. I was so afraid that there were weeks when I'd just stay home and not go to the park because I didn't want to get hurt.

But as much as we would love to distance ourselves from such people, God says to still love them even though they may not like us. It sounds like a hard thing to do, but it's a command God gave us. He said if you only like people who already like you, you can't stand out from someone who doesn't know Jesus. He wants you to be different from everybody so that your life can display the gospel to those who see you.

In the Old Testament, there was a rule that said, "Love your neighbor and hate your enemy," but then Jesus said to love your enemies and pray for those who persecute you. Hate cannot be in the heart of the Christian because that is not the character of God—God Himself is love.

*"You have heard that it was said, 'Love your neighbor and hate your enemy.' But I tell you, love your enemies and pray for those who persecute you."*

**Matthew 5:43–44**

## Reflect

*Would you ever mistreat yourself or someone you love? The Bible says love your enemies the same way you love yourself. What do you think that means? It might be difficult to love someone who makes you feel bad, but I'll let you in on a little secret: Often the people who try to hurt you intentionally do it because they are feeling hurt by reasons unrelated to you, and they are just lashing out. So, by offering them compassion and love despite their behavior, you may be helping them.*

## Respond

*Can you think of a time when you got really upset with someone? Maybe you got into a disagreement with a classmate, or your dog destroyed your shoes and made you really angry. Think about that time and when you're ready, come back to this page and answer these questions:*

**What happened?**

____________________________________________

____________________________________________

____________________________________________

**I remember these people were there:** ________________

____________________________________________

____________________________________________

____________________________________________

**How did I feel after that happened?**

*Now imagine if this took place today. Ask yourself if you would say or do anything differently, now that you are older and wiser. Think about that time and what you'd do differently now, then, come back to this page and answer these questions:*

**Now that I've thought about this again, how could I have shown more love in the situation?**

**How would being a more loving person have made what happened a better experience for me?**

**When I look ahead to next week, I can be a more loving person by:**

CONTINUED ON NEXT PAGE ➡

CONTINUED FROM PREVIOUS PAGE

*This exercise will really show you how you've become more Christ-like. It's also a good way to practice "injecting" more love into your daily life. By approaching your enemies with a kind and loving heart, you will better yourself as a son of God.*

Thank you, Lord, for your word. I am grateful to be your son. Please help me love people the same way you do. Amen.

# ASK GOD FOR WISDOM!

A lot of Christians forget that God is their father. Many Christians forget that God's wisdom is always available to them because they are His children. If you're a child and God is your father, when you need advice all you have to do is ask, and He will guide you. The Bible says, "Ask and it shall be given to you, seek and you will find, knock and the door will be open." You should always have that mindset that you can ask God anything because you have a right as His child.

King Solomon became the wisest king on the earth when he simply asked God to guide him. He realized he was a little boy who could possibly make mistakes leading the kingdom, and he asked God to help him make the right decisions so he didn't destroy what his father had built. God was so happy that Solomon didn't ask Him for money or the most power, so He told Solomon that he would be the wisest and the greatest among any other kings.

The same way Solomon was just a young boy who asked God for wisdom to make the right decisions, you're never too young to make this same request. God wants you to be wise, so that you can follow in His footsteps and be great. Wisdom is taking what God has said and applying it to your life.

*If any of you lacks wisdom, you should ask God, who gives generously to all without finding fault, and it will be given to you.*

**James 1:5**

## Reflect

*God wants you to be able to make wise decisions in your life so you don't mistakenly go down the wrong path. His wisdom is available to you if you're willing to ask Him for it.*

## Respond

*Each morning before you go to school this week, write down a piece of good advice you've received during your life and try to put it into practice.*

1. ______________________________
2. ______________________________
3. ______________________________
4. ______________________________
5. ______________________________

*On the weekend, think about two questions you have for God where you could really use His wisdom. Write them down here, and then trust He will soon reveal the answers you need.*

1. ______________________________
2. ______________________________

> Father God, today I ask you to fill me with the spirit of wisdom so that I can make the right decisions in my life. Amen.

# PRAY JUST LIKE JESUS TAUGHT

In my early years following Jesus, I had a problem with praying because I would always be done in 15 seconds. I knew I had to talk to God, but I didn't know how to and how long we were supposed to talk for. Luckily, I wasn't alone in this. In the gospel of Luke, Jesus's disciples also asked him to teach them how to pray. They literally had the best teacher on earth and so do we—we have Jesus's words in the Bible and the Holy Spirit.

When Jesus starts his prayer, he says **"Father, hallowed be your name."** In other words, always start off your prayers honoring God by thanking Him and praising His name because He is mighty and there is power in His name to save us. Jesus then states, **"Your kingdom come and your will be done."** With these words, he is asking that God do whatever He wants to do for that day, moment, or time period, and we will accept it and do our best to follow it. Next, Jesus says, **"Give us our daily bread,"** because God is the one who feeds us at all cost, and we need to acknowledge that. Have you heard the story of Jesus turning five loaves of bread into enough to feed 5,000 people? It's amazing! At the end of the prayer, Jesus says, **"Forgive us our sins, for we also forgive everyone who sins against us, and lead us not into temptation."** This means we should ask God for forgiveness anytime we pray and ask Him to help us avoid doing things we know He wouldn't approve of.

Jesus taught us to pray this way because he knew we would need it during the times when we aren't sure what to say to God.

*One day Jesus was praying in a certain place. When he finished, one of his disciples said to him, "Lord, teach us to pray, just as John taught his disciples."*

**Luke 11:1**

## Reflect

*Whenever you feel stuck while praying, you can use this outline from Jesus. When you start it this way, the Holy Spirit will also empower you to speak to God even more.*

## Respond

*Just like any skill, the more you practice praying, the better you'll get at it. You can use this outline to begin your prayers each morning and evening, or you can come up with your own prayers and write them below. If you start to pray every day, it will build your faith and give you confidence to have regular conversations with God.*

Lord, as I follow your formula of prayer, help me make communication with you a habit in my life. Amen.

# WHAT YOU WATCH MATTERS TO GOD

Your eyes are so powerful, and they can be used for either good or evil. Why? Because whatever your eyes see is what you start to think about. If you see good things, that's what you think about, but if you constantly see bad things, you might start to focus on them.

When I was younger, I was always around sports. All I ever wanted to do was play sports—I thought about them all day at school and even dreamed about them at night. But let's turn the situation around for a second. My friends used to live in a pretty dangerous neighborhood where terrible things, like stealing, happened often. If stealing is what you always see, you're going to start thinking about it all the time—and eventually you'll probably act on your thoughts, which can really get you in trouble.

The things you see are important, and you're the one who is ultimately in control of what you watch on TV or online. If you have to turn something off when your parents come into the room, then you know it's wrong. Television networks don't care if what you see is appropriate—they only care about entertainment. So you need to make sure you're only watching things that reflect the good of God. Be like the man Job in the Old Testament, who promised to never look at anything bad ever again.

*"The eye is the lamp of the body. If your eyes are healthy, your whole body will be full of light."*

**Matthew 6:22**

## Reflect

*Your eyes are supposed to shine a bright light to your heart and guide you through the darkness. So try to think about things that will help you share the light of God with the world and help you be an agent of light. If you have any movies or games that feature bad content, let your parents know.*

## Respond

*Make a list of seven TV shows or movies that you think shine a positive light on the world. Before you watch anything this week, look back over your list and think about whether the thing you're planning to watch would fit in this list.*

1. ______________________________
2. ______________________________
3. ______________________________
4. ______________________________
5. ______________________________
6. ______________________________
7. ______________________________

> Lord, I confess my wrongs to you and ask for forgiveness of my sins. I promise to be careful of what I let my eyes see so that I can remain pure for you. Amen.

# BE A HARD WORKER

A lot of people don't like the idea of hard work because they think it isn't fun. But look at LeBron James, one of the greatest basketball players ever—how do you think he got there? Hard work. He wasn't lazy and sitting around saying, "I'm so tall, so obviously I'm going to be the greatest." He worked harder than everyone around him to get to the top of his game, and now he's extremely successful. Nothing happens by chance or accident.

The Bible says that if you just dream without doing anything, you're chasing a fantasy that's never going to happen. The book of James says that faith without work is dead. You can't have a master plan of changing the world and then put no action toward it. A wise man named Frederick Douglass talked about how he stopped praying on his knees and started praying with his feet. In other words, he stopped sitting around hoping for something to happen and instead got up and made change happen.

As a child of God, you have to be a hard worker because, if you aren't, how will you be able to take care of your loved ones or even yourself? How will you be able to give to charities or change the world like we discussed earlier in this devotional? Hard work is the attitude of a winner—and that's exactly what you are. You just have to show the world your determination so that they can see you as a winner too!

***Those who work their land will have abundant food, but those who chase fantasies have no sense.***

**Proverbs 12:11**

## Reflect

*The difference between the wise and the unwise is that the wise work hard to follow God's instructions and make His greatness a reality in their lives.*

## Respond

*Now is the perfect time to begin your journey to greatness. Think about a time when you worked really hard and saw great success from your big effort, like a good grade on a big school project, or earning money for doing extra chores. Write on the lines below about how that felt. Then, make a plan for how you can show the same courage this week. Write that down too.*

God, help me be a hard worker and someone who values those who also work hard. In Jesus's name. Amen.

# YOU ARE THE LIGHT OF THE WORLD

I was around 12 years old when I first accepted Jesus as my Lord and personal savior, and I was extremely excited to let everyone know. But I was also scared because I didn't want my friends and family to look at me differently. I went to a public school, so religion wasn't a big thing, and nobody really talked about it. But I wanted to share what Jesus did for me with people everywhere.

Anytime we were playing basketball or soccer, I'd talk about church and all the fun I had there with my church friends. Then I'd invite others to church with me, and because of the personal relationships I had with them, they would always come and enjoy themselves. God was working on their hearts, and they started sharing more about Jesus with their families and friends.

Because I was very young, I didn't want to tell people the wrong information, so I used to take my friends to church and let the older Christians explain Jesus to them. We are all called to be a light to the world and share the gospel with other people we see every day. This is one of the reasons you were created—to tell people about Jesus and his love for me and you.

*He said to them, "Go into all the world and preach the gospel to all creation."*

**Mark 16:15**

## Reflect

*I know it's a scary thing to talk to people about someone you may not have physically seen. But you know deep down how real Jesus is to you, so don't let the fear of others stop you from being a light to the world.*

## Respond

*This week, look for opportunities to have a conversation about these things with three of the people you are closest to. Write their names in below. It's always easier to start with people you know well, but with practice, you'll be able to talk to almost anyone about Jesus.*

1. ______________________________
2. ______________________________
3. ______________________________

God, thank you for your salvation. Give me the boldness to be able to share the gospel with others and truly be a light in this dark world. Amen.

# REMEMBER TO DO YOUR CHORES

Let's be honest here: Almost nobody likes doing chores. My parents would always tell me to go sweep the kitchen when I was watching TV. I'd tell them I'd do it after the show was over, but then I'd always forget and get in trouble. This happened over and over again, until I eventually realized it was all my fault. If I just did my chores without them asking me to do them, I would never get in trouble or hear any complaints.

Believe it or not, having chores is a good thing because they help you build responsibility and prepare you for the real world. When you grow up to be an adult, you're not going to have someone telling you all the time to go and clean up. So if you don't have the mature mind to go and do it yourself, the place you live in will look like a complete disaster. Nobody wants to live in a messy house or with a messy person who doesn't take responsibility.

When you do your chores, you feel a sense of accomplishment because you turned something that was dirty into something clean. You have the ability to transform so many things. I know you still may not enjoy it, but the Bible says that whatever you do, do it without complaining because it's for the glory of God. Yes, doing your chores is pleasing to God because you're obeying your parents, and you're doing something instead of just sitting on your couch watching TV or playing games.

*Children, obey your parents in all things:*
*for this is well pleasing unto the Lord.*

**Colossians 3:20 KJV**

## Reflect

*Remember that everything you're asked to do is for a reason. So do it the way you would if God asked you—do it for His glory and without grumbling or arguing.*

## Respond

*On at least two days this week, find a chore that needs to be done and do it without anyone asking you. While you're doing it, think about how satisfying it is to take responsibility to help out around the house without your parents telling you to. You could also write down some ideas here for other chores you can help out with on a regular basis.*

God, thank you for the lessons you show me through your word. Help me be obedient to my parents and hardworking. Amen.

# DREAM BIG—NOTHING IS IMPOSSIBLE WITH GOD!

Someone once told me that if my dreams don't scare me, they aren't big enough. I really sat down and thought about how true that is. A dream that doesn't scare you is a dream you can easily do by yourself without any hard work, which means anyone can accomplish it.

I want you to dream so big that you know you're going to need God to help you achieve it. Maybe it's to win the Stanley Cup? Or to be the youngest entrepreneur to earn a million dollars? Or to be the youngest astronaut to fly up into space? Or to find a way to make sure every person in the world has access to clean, fresh water? God loves it when people dream bigger than might seem realistically possible, and they can't reach their goals by themselves. They need to ask God for help. He can do anything and He has no limitations. He loves it when His children come to Him because He is the God of the impossible. Nothing is too hard for Him. Dream the biggest dream ever and ask God to come into the picture, and see what He does to help you!

One night, Joseph had a dream that one day many people would bow down to him. He told his brothers about the dream, and they got really angry at him because they thought he was implying that he was better than all of them. In fact, they were so offended that they decided to sell him to traveling merchants. Joseph might have thought there was no possible way that his dream could come true now. But this was all part of God's plan. He allowed Joseph to go through such trials because He was preparing him for when his dream would come true.

It's easy to think that when we have a dream, it will happen exactly the way we imagine it should. But God takes everyone along a unique route so that everyone's personal encounter with Him is different—that way nobody can say that they know God's formula. Do you know what happened to Joseph? He became the prime minister—the second in charge—of the very same land where he was imprisoned. People ended up bowing down to Joseph in the same way he had seen in his dream, and his brothers were among those people. God can make anything possible, as long as you follow the route He has chosen specially for you. Just believe and walk with God all the way.

*For with God nothing shall be impossible.*

**Luke 1:37 KJV**

## Reflect

*If you never dream or have hope for anything, you will never be able to see God create a wonderful miracle in your life.*

## Respond

*Write down three of your biggest dreams here:*

*Now ask yourself the following questions about each of these dreams:*

*What is one small step I can take now toward achieving this dream? (For example, maybe you could work harder on your ice-skating skills, or learn all you can about astronomy.)*

---

---

*Who in my life, along with God, can help me work toward this dream and hold me accountable?*

---

---

*Who is a role model I admire who has already achieved a similar dream? What can I learn from them, even though my path will be different?*

---

---

You are a God who can make the impossible possible. Thank you for allowing me to experience your power in my life. Amen.

# ALWAYS GIVE GOD YOUR BEST

Do you know the story of the brothers Cain and Abel? Abel loved Cain, but Cain hated Abel. Throughout the story, we learn that Abel was a good young boy who really loved the Lord and wanted to please Him in everything he did. But Cain lived his own life and didn't care much about anything or anyone but himself.

The time came when the two brothers were supposed to bring their sacrifices to God like their parents had taught them. Cain brought God some fruits and vegetables that he farmed from the ground, while Abel brought fat portions of meat from his barn to sacrifice to God. God was really happy with Abel but disappointed with Cain. Abel's sacrifice was worthy of God because he looked for the very best thing he could give to show how important and powerful God was. But when Cain thought he could just give some veggies that would rot in a few days, he didn't really show any care for God—and God didn't appreciate that.

If your teacher gives you an assignment, do it like you're doing it for God and give it your best shot. Remember how I said to do everything for the glory of God? That means whether you're taking out the garbage, cooking a meal, or working on a project for school, always give your best effort. If you see other people not giving their best, don't let that be an excuse—it just means you'll stand out even more as a child of God.

*In the course of time Cain brought some of the fruits of the soil as an offering to the Lord. And Abel also brought an offering—fat portions from some of the firstborn of his flock. The Lord looked with favor on Abel and his offering.*

**Genesis 4:3–4**

## Reflect

*Is there anything you have been holding back on that you know you could do better? Are you really giving your best to God in everything that you do?*

## Respond

*Think about five things you could do this week with more effort than usual to show that you are giving God your all. List them below so that you can refer back to them each day.*

1. ______________________________
2. ______________________________
3. ______________________________
4. ______________________________
5. ______________________________

God, I thank you for showing me that I need to do better. Help me give you my all in everything that I do. Amen.

# WHY CAN'T WE BE FRIENDS?

I have two older sisters and two younger brothers, so I'm the middle child. It definitely feels weird whenever there's a fight because I never know whose side to be on. My older sister and I never really got along for years. I used to annoy her a lot, and I loved doing it. As I got older and started to mature, things got better between us, and I realized how great it is for a family to live in unity and harmony.

I know every family has their issues, and no family is perfect. But if you try, you can all get along with each other. It's a beautiful thing to see when family members are also friends. God says He loves unity because that's what He represents in heaven. The father, son, and Holy Spirit are always in perfect unity at all times. You have to strive to be more like they are up there so you never have to face problems down here.

Have you ever been on a fun vacation with all your family members? You probably took photos, right? I like to say that a family picture where everybody is smiling and happy is a photograph that represents God. You are supposed to be a mirror of how God is with the son and with the Holy Spirit. They have been together since the beginning of time, and nothing has been able to separate them. It's important that you aim to find the same love and unity with your own family here on earth, even if it takes some effort!

*"How good and pleasant it is when God's people live together in unity!"*

**Psalm 133:1**

## Reflect

*Have you ever heard the saying, "There's strength in numbers"? Well, there is also strength in unity. A strong team doesn't just mean having a lot of players—it means having players who work together as one and appreciate each other.*

## Respond

*Think about the people in your life who you may not get along with as well as you could. Then make an effort to reach out to each one and talk about how you can overcome your differences and forgive each other. It's okay if you can only think of a few people—that means you're already doing a good job building unity with people in your family, school, and church. Use the lines below to make a list and organize your thoughts.*

Father, help me be more like you. Help me bring people together and display your power through unity. In Jesus's name. Amen.

# ALWAYS FOLLOW THE GOLDEN RULE

Jesus said to do to others what you would want them to do to you. They call this the golden rule because "gold" carries a lot of value, and it is awesome to show such care and respect for your fellow neighbor or friend. The golden rule has become universal for almost every religion, school, and workplace. This is the standard every person tries to live up to, and even though we often fall short, it's still an attainable goal, especially when you have the Holy Spirit living inside you. You have to learn how to live a life that is selfless because that is where you get your reward from God.

Whenever you do something, think about whether it's what you would want someone to do to you. Jesus also said to love your neighbor as you love yourself. This means showing compassion by asking a friend, "Hey, how are you doing?" and really listening to the answer. Or offering forgiveness when someone makes a mistake, because nobody is perfect. It's important to show the love of God at all times. Realistically speaking, that's not an easy thing to do, but you have to work toward it and get better every day. Look at it this way—if you and some friends made fun of someone at school, would you like it if someone did that to you with a bunch of their friends? On the flip side, if you gave someone a nice snack when they were hungry, wouldn't you like it if somebody did that to you? I know I sure would.

*So in everything, do to others what you would have them do to you, for this sums up the Law and the Prophets.*

**Matthew 7:12**

## Reflect

*The golden rule is the key to a fulfilling life. Treat others how you want to be treated. Forget about the negative things they might have done to you in the past and instead focus on their humanity. Treat them with the same respect and love you would like to receive.*

## Respond

*Each day this week, look for one nice thing you could do for someone that would make you happy if they did it for you. This could be giving up your seat on the bus, holding the door open for someone, or even helping your parent make dinner so that they have more time to relax. At the end of the week, write down how it felt to live by this universal rule.*

---

---

---

Thank you, God, for teaching us the golden rule. Help us make it our lifestyle in Jesus's name. Amen.

# DON'T BE AFRAID—GOD IS ALWAYS WITH YOU

Have you ever felt lonely even though there were many people around you? That feeling happens to a lot of us in our lives, especially me. Before my two younger brothers were born, I was the only boy in my family. I have two older sisters, and they would always do everything together and leave me out of it. I didn't really have anyone to go to, so I'd always be by myself. Sometimes feeling lonely can make you act out because you feel like people don't understand you. I get it—and it's not your fault. It's normal to feel that way. But in times like these, remember that even though you may feel alone, God sees you, He hears you, and He understands you.

When you're feeling lonely, God says to not worry because He has always been with you, and He will never forsake you. For some people, being lonely is scary, and they are afraid of how others may treat them if they go to a new school or move to a new city. But God is ready to strengthen you and lift you up. He will never let you be embarrassed or ever leave you alone. Trust in Him always and don't be afraid to call on His name. He is your heavenly father who is where you are any time of the day. He is the reason you are alive and well today, so whenever you have fears, talk to Him about them, and He will save you. God is always with you.

*"So do not fear, for I am with you; do not be dismayed, for I am your God. I will strengthen you and help you; I will uphold you with my righteous right hand."*

**Isaiah 41:10**

## Reflect

*If God says that you shouldn't be afraid, take that in full confidence. Trust Him when He says He will strengthen you, help you, and uplift you.*

## Respond

*At the beginning of this week, write down two of your biggest fears and then take them to God each day in prayer to ask Him for guidance.*

1. ______________________________

2. ______________________________

*At the end of the week, note if you feel any different, knowing that God is always with you even when you feel alone.*

1. ______________________________

2. ______________________________

Thank you, God, for your word. I bring my fears before you and ask that you strengthen me, help me overcome, and lift me up to a place of righteousness. Amen.

WEEK 29

# BE THE GOOD SAMARITAN

Often when you do something nice for somebody—like helping someone cross the road or buying hot chocolate on a cold day for a stranger—you are called a Good Samaritan. To some people, a Good Samaritan is just a kind person who does nice things for others when it is convenient for them. But when you look into this parable Jesus taught, it's a little bit deeper than that.

Some time ago, the Jews didn't like Samaritans at all because they were considered to be outcasts and disobedient people. The Jews had a really hard time getting along with them because some Samaritans destroyed the Jewish temple where they worshiped God, and they were really angry about it. But Jesus tells a story about a Jewish man going down from Jerusalem to Jericho who got robbed and beaten up along the way. Two different priests walked by him and left him there to die, but a Samaritan, whom they hated, came and helped him by cleaning and bandaging his wounds and taking him to a hotel to be safe.

Most people would think that the priests were supposed to help, especially since they were both Jews. But instead, the person who they all hated saw this hurt man and had compassion for him.

> *But a Samaritan, as he traveled, came where the man was; and when he saw him, he took pity on him. He went to him and bandaged his wounds, pouring on oil and wine. Then he put the man on his own donkey, brought him to an inn and took care of him.*
>
> **Luke 10:33–34**

## Reflect

*We live in a world today where people only care about themselves. Jesus gives you a hard task to love those who don't really love you. How can you truly be a Good Samaritan where you are today?*

## Respond

*When you see anyone in need this week, and you can help them, make the effort to do it without expecting anything back in return. At the end of the week, write down what you were able to accomplish as a Good Samaritan.*

God, help me be someone who loves people despite what they may think of me. Help me be a true Good Samaritan. Amen.

# FIND YOUR GOD-GIVEN STRENGTHS

Samson was a man with super strength that God gave him because of the promises his parents kept to God before he was born. An angel appeared to his mother and told her that her future son would be a lifelong Nazirite dedicated to the service of God. But there was a rule that he must never drink alcohol or cut off his hair, because his hair was the secret to his strength. Though Samson's power was given by God, he always relied on his own strength to defeat his enemies throughout his life. After he started seeing how much he could do on his own, pride started to build up in his heart. He disobeyed God by marrying someone he wasn't supposed to, and that's where everything went wrong for him.

God chose Samson to accomplish a very specific task and that's why He made him a Nazirite. But Samson decided to go his own way and got distracted, falling in love with a woman named Delilah who ruined his whole life. She trapped him by pretending she loved him and then let soldiers cut off his hair while he was sleeping. Samson lost his strength for some time after his hair was cut, but when he called on the name of the Lord, God heard him. He gave Samson strength one last time to accomplish his mission to defeat the Philistines who were enemies of God's people. When Samson trusted God and asked him for strength, he achieved the greatest victory in his life and fulfilled his life's purpose.

*Samson said, "Let me die with the Philistines!" Then he pushed with all his might, and down came the temple on the rulers and all the people in it. Thus he killed many more when he died than while he lived.*

**Judges 16:30**

## Reflect

*Sometimes our pride can get the better of us. But you can learn from Samson's mistakes and strive to always be who God says you are, following His will and His way, and walking in the strength He has given to you.*

## Respond

*For the first half of this week, think about the strengths God has given you and how you can use them to do good in the world. Write them here.*

CONTINUED ON NEXT PAGE ➡

CONTINUED FROM PREVIOUS PAGE

*For the rest of the week, consider your weaknesses and write down how you think God can help you turn them into strengths.*

Thank you, God, for strengthening me to do your will. Help me always follow you. Amen.

# GOD CARES ABOUT YOUR HEALTH

How important is a healthy lifestyle to you? Do you want to live a long time and still be active when you're older? Do you want to be able to do well in gym class? Well, God cares about your health too. He wants you to be healthy and strong so that you don't get sick or injured. A lot of people get sick because they don't focus on the two main things that will help them stay fit: exercise and healthy eating.

When you exercise, you make your body stronger. Just about every guy on the face of this planet wants to be strong, and I'm guessing you do too. Your heart is very important and you need to take care of it. It works really hard to pump your blood throughout your body. So how do you make your heart stronger? By doing things that make you breathe harder, like swimming, running, or playing basketball, soccer, or hockey. You can also strengthen your muscles by regularly doing things like push-ups, sit-ups, and jumping jacks.

Eating healthy means eating a variety of foods so that you get all the nutrients you need for normal growth. Everyone's body reacts to food differently, so you'll need to figure out what works best for you to get the most benefits. But the foods that are most likely to help you stay healthy and grow stronger are fruits and veggies, whole grains like pasta and rice, and milk (dairy or non-dairy).

*Dear friend, I pray that you may enjoy good health and that all may go well with you, even as your soul is getting along well.*

**3 John 1:2**

## Reflect

*If you want to fulfill God's purpose in your life, you need to be healthy and strong so you're able to share His word with others. What change are you making today?*

## Respond

*Make a list of healthy grocery items and ask your parents if they can buy them for you this week.*

*Now make a list of three activities you can do this week that will get your heart pumping or strengthen your muscles.*

Thank you, Lord, for giving me good health. I promise to continue to take care of it, and I pray you help those who are sick and bring healing to them. Amen.

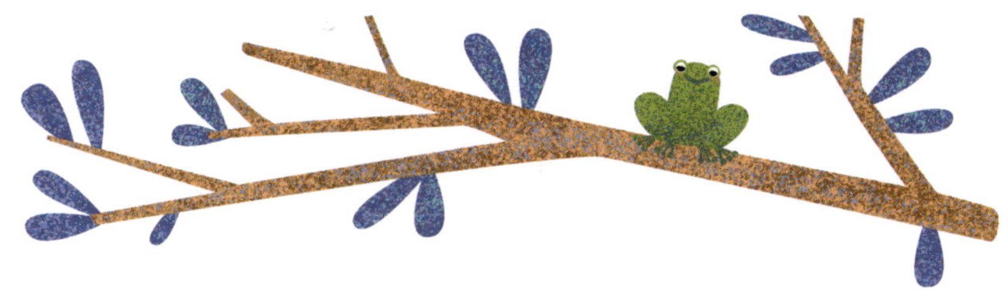

# WHAT DO YOU KNOW ABOUT HEAVEN?

There's a story about a young boy who, while having surgery, said he went to heaven and saw Jesus. He saw and heard the things his parents were saying to God and the groups of people praying in the room—he even saw his sister who had already died. When the surgery was over, the boy returned to his body and told his father what he had witnessed—and it turned out that everything he saw and heard really happened.

Though I can't tell you if this is 100 percent true, I can tell you heaven is definitely real because that's God's kingdom. The Bible talks about how we are going to go to heaven one day and spend our life forever with God. It might sound unbelievable, but that's God's promise to us. So what's so great about heaven?

**Heaven will be fun!** Imagine spending time forever with the creator of heaven and earth. We have fun when we take trips or go to the park, but imagine talking with the person who made that amazing park and having a real friendship with Him.

**Heaven is a real place.** The Bible talks about how there will be streets of gold and how Jesus has mansions and houses prepared for us. Imagine that.

**We will be perfect in heaven.** Jesus was perfect on earth and is surely perfect in heaven. We will never have to worry about dishonoring God in heaven because we will have reached perfection when we get there, and we will all be like Jesus.

Sounds like an amazing thing to be chosen to join, right?

*My Father's house has many rooms; if that were not so, would I have told you that I am going there to prepare a place for you?*

**John 14:2**

## Reflect

*Do you want to make it to this place called heaven? There's one sure way to get there: Dedicate your life to living God's purpose, being His light in the world, and asking for His forgiveness when you make mistakes.*

## Respond

*Write down your sins here and then use your prayers this week to ask God for forgiveness.*

God, I know where you are is awesome, and I want to be where you are forever. Help me get there. Amen.

# WATCH WHAT YOU SAY

King Solomon's proverbs have a lot of wisdom that can help keep you out of trouble. A preacher by the name of Billy Graham once said that because there were 31 days in the month, and there are also 31 chapters in proverbs, he would read one chapter and five psalms a day. It might be too much for you right now, but as you get older, you'll see how important that really is. Billy Graham said he read those psalms to build his relationship with God, but he read proverbs to improve his relationship with his friends, family, and people in general. It's not enough just to focus on the spiritual aspect of your faith—you have to also focus on your self-development so you can be strong in every area of your life.

King Solomon says if you watch what you say, and guard your tongue, you'll never find yourself in trouble. When I was around your age, I used to get in trouble because of the things I said. I didn't know how to keep secrets and always said things at the wrong times. Many of us feel like we'll burst if we keep stuff inside of us, but the Bible says that it's wise to watch what we say because we might be misunderstood. I'm not telling you to hide every single thing, but I am saying that you need to know when to talk and when to keep quiet.

Learning to keep your mouth closed will get you far in life because it means you have self-control and don't need to spread other people's secrets. Live a quiet and humble life, not getting yourself, or other people, into trouble.

*Those who guard their mouths and their tongues*
*keep themselves from calamity.*

**Proverbs 21:23**

## Reflect

*Commit yourself to only saying positive things and not spreading other people's information without their permission. That will help you guard your mouth and keep yourself away from trouble.*

## Respond

*Take notice this week of when you feel the urge to talk about other people behind their backs or share their secrets. Write a list of positive things you could say instead.*

God, help me have better self-control and not say things that will get me in trouble. Help me be wise and live how you ask me to in your word. Amen.

# DON'T EVER STOP GROWING

I know this may sound weird, but some people choose to stop growing. I don't mean physically, but mentally and spiritually. As a young boy reading this book, you are close to becoming a teenager, which means you're physically becoming taller, stronger, and bigger. But if you had a way to look inside your mind or spirit, you would see that they don't automatically grow as you get older. They grow because you decide to nourish them. You have to choose to grow your mind and spirit. As we've already discussed, nobody becomes great by accident. It takes a lot of effort and hard work, and you have to practice more than once a week.

You can help your mind grow by reading books from the library or online. Make sure you always do your homework so that you really understand the subject you're studying in school. And ask your teachers and other adults plenty of questions about the world so that you can explore new topics. When you start exploring new things, you might find topics you're really interested in learning about that you can also share with others in your school, church, or home.

Now is the perfect time to start creating learning habits that will benefit you for the rest of your life—think of it as investing in your future. It will lead you to success, which is what God wants for you.

*But grow in the grace and knowledge of our Lord and Savior Jesus Christ. To him be glory both now and forever! Amen.*

**2 Peter 3:18**

## Reflect

*Growing is a choice you make. In the same way your physical body needs nourishment from the right foods, so does your spiritual body. Be mindful of what you put into it and make sure you feed it with things that will help it grow.*

## Respond

*Each day this week, focus on one thing you can do to feed your spiritual body and write it down here. Keep this list handy so that you can refer back to it throughout the year. Make sure you are continually learning and growing.*

God, help me choose to grow more every day in the grace and knowledge of Jesus. Amen.

# YOU HAVE INDEPENDENCE IN GOD

Being independent is a big responsibility. God gave us the independence to live our lives because He doesn't want to control us. If He did, we'd be robots and not human beings who can make our own choices. God trusts you enough to make the right decisions; He said it in His word. The only thing He asks of us is that we don't use our freedom to do evil things to other people or ourselves. Many people have freedom, but they abuse it, which explains why so many terrible things are happening in the world today. We are responsible for the decisions we make every single day and the consequences that come with them.

Independence means having freedom. I know as a young boy, you probably want freedom at home from your parents or your siblings. But since they don't know your heart or mind the way God does, you'll have to show them that you are worthy of that independence. Here are a few ways you can do that:

- Take responsibility for some extra chores around the house.
- Make your own schedule and follow it.
- Learn to think for yourself.
- Volunteer at church or anywhere else.

*Live as free people, but do not use your freedom as a cover-up for evil.*

**1 Peter 2:16**

## Reflect

*Independence comes with a lot of responsibility, and you have to be willing to show others that you're walking down that path. Make changes to your life that will show your friends and family how responsible you are.*

## Respond

*At the dinner table, ask your family members if there are things you could do to improve yourself. You might not like the answers at first, because constructive criticism can be tough to hear—but it's how you become more responsible. Here are some questions you could ask:*

*What is something I did this week that showed I could be responsible?*

___

___

*What is something I need to improve on so that I can show you how responsible I can be?*

___

___

*How can I be more helpful around the house?*

___

___

CONTINUED ON NEXT PAGE ➡

CONTINUED FROM PREVIOUS PAGE

*For the rest of this week, think about your family's answers and how you can incorporate the feedback into your daily behavior.*

Use the space below to write down your thoughts.

God, thank you for your freedom. Please help me live out my life the way you want me to and be a responsible person with the freedom you have given me. Amen.

# YOUR FAITH CAN MOVE MOUNTAINS

Jesus said that if you have faith as small as a mustard seed, you can tell a mountain to move and it will move. And it's true.

There was a time when Jesus's disciples were trying to heal someone from an evil spirit, and they kept trying and trying but nothing was happening. Jesus had to come and heal the little boy himself. Later he told his disciples that their faith was too small. So just imagine that. Jesus says the faith of a mustard seed can move mountains, but the faith of the disciples still didn't work when they were trying to heal that young boy. When you have a moment, look up how small a mustard seed is—it's tiny! So that means the disciples' faith was microscopic in comparison.

But God says that even with the smallest amount of faith, you can make things happen in your life when you put your trust in Him. God can make the impossible possible if you just believe that He will do it. Though Jesus was saying that you only need a small amount of faith, I want to encourage you to have really large faith. From today, start dreaming the biggest dreams for what you want in life and have faith that God will help you accomplish it.

Do you want to make the basketball team? Get really good at the guitar? Or be a better sibling to your brothers and sisters? Start believing that you can do it and have faith in God that He will help you accomplish it. Remember that Jesus said that if you believe, it will happen, and if there's anyone in this world you can trust, it's Jesus. Do you know what the Bible says faith is? It says that faith is confidence in something you hope for but cannot necessarily see. So even though you can't see it, you're still hoping for it.

So keep on hoping and keep on believing, because God is ready to respond to your faith. Are you ready for some amazing things to happen in your life? I'm extremely excited for you!

> *"Because you have so little faith. Truly I tell you, if you have faith as small as a mustard seed, you can say to this mountain, 'Move from here to there,' and it will move. Nothing will be impossible for you."*
>
> **Matthew 17:20**

## Reflect

*Though only a small amount of faith is required to move a mountain, imagine if you had gigantic faith. God acts according to your faith because when you trust Him, it gives Him permission to do what you asked Him to do. If you have gigantic faith, you'll be able to join that school club or sports team you want to. God is supporting you in everything you do. Faith gives you the power to do the impossible.*

## Respond

*Each day this week, write down one way you'd like God to show up in your life. Maybe you have a big test at school, or you have an ill relative and you want them to get better. Then, think of one prayer you can say to ask the Lord for his guidance and help. Can you see His action and love in your daily life?*

**Day 1**

*What help do I need?*

*What prayer can I say?*

**Day 2**

*What help do I need?*

*What prayer can I say?*

**Day 3**

*What help do I need?*

*What prayer can I say?*

CONTINUED ON NEXT PAGE ➡

CONTINUED FROM PREVIOUS PAGE

**Day 4**

*What help do I need?*

*What prayer can I say?*

**Day 5**

*What help do I need?*

*What prayer can I say?*

**Day 6**

*What help do I need?*

*What prayer can I say?*

**Day 7**

*What help do I need?*

*What prayer can I say?*

God, thank you for helping me believe. Please increase my faith and help me have faith that is bigger than a mustard seed. Amen.

# OBEDIENCE IS BETTER THAN SACRIFICE

There are many times in our lives where we think we are doing things that will make God happy. But the only way God is truly happy with us is when we follow what He has told us to do.

In the book of Samuel, the Israelites were very quick to give sacrifices to God in order to earn His approval. They'd give things like goats, lambs, or pigeons and ask for forgiveness of their sins, or blessings from God. This became so much of a habit that they didn't even care when they sinned because they knew they could always offer a sacrifice to God and ask for forgiveness. Because that was the law God made, He accepted many of their sacrifices. But they didn't truly care about God or their relationship with Him—they just wanted what God could give them.

Many people behave this way, thinking that if they give their money to God and the church, that's all they need to do to make Him happy. But that's not how God really works. In fact, He told King Saul, through the prophet Samuel, that it's better to obey Him than to just keep sacrificing all the time. God wants a relationship with His people—He wants them to know Him the same way He knows them. So it's important to remember that the path to heaven is carved by obedience to God and His gospel. We can walk this path by doing things like helping the poor, volunteering at church, reading the Bible, and praying every day. We can only get to heaven by obeying the word of the Lord and putting our trust in Jesus.

*But Samuel replied: "Does the Lord delight in burnt offerings and sacrifices as much as in obeying the Lord? To obey is better than sacrifice, and to heed is better than the fat of rams."*

**1 Samuel 15:22**

## Reflect

*Choose to follow God and to be obedient to His word, his will and his way. Your obedience is better than any sacrifice.*

## Respond

*Think of ways you can make obeying God a daily habit. Each morning when you wake up this week, write down a way you plan to show your obedience to God that day, whether it's reading the Bible, volunteering, or helping someone who needs it.*

***Day 1***

*To show my obedience to God today, I will:*

---

***Day 2***

*To show my obedience to God today, I will:*

---

***Day 3***

*To show my obedience to God today, I will:*

---

CONTINUED ON NEXT PAGE ➨

CONTINUED FROM PREVIOUS PAGE

**Day 4**

*To show my obedience to God today, I will:*

---

**Day 5**

*To show my obedience to God today, I will:*

---

**Day 6**

*To show my obedience to God today, I will:*

---

**Day 7**

*To show my obedience to God today, I will:*

---

God, help me to not do things my way but to honor you and obey you in everything that I do, in Jesus's name. Amen.

# GOD IS LOOKING FOR YOU!

Believe it or not, there was a time in history where the people on earth decided to distance themselves from God and everything associated with Him. There was no one around to try to bring peace to the world, and everything had broken down into complete chaos. God looked everywhere to find someone who could be His representative here on earth and for the people of Israel. He needed just one person to stand in the gap and build the wall of righteousness that guarded the land so there would be no more harm. But He couldn't even find one person.

I always ask myself, how many people were really there? The truth is, the nation of Israel was full of many people, but nobody was willing to be chosen for the task. They preferred to live in unrighteousness and stay silent and let the chaos continue to happen right before their eyes. No one was brave enough to stand up and take responsibility for sharing the light of God and all its goodness.

I chose this Bible story because it makes me think of our world today. It feels like we're faced with more challenges than ever, and we're becoming even more disconnected from one another. So many people are addicted to their phones, and they ignore their loved ones who are right in front of them. Others want to be validated by social media even though they may not even know the people on the other side of the screen. While they may not say it out loud, many people are desperate, lonely, and hurting, and they don't know what to do about it.

Among all this chaos, God is looking for someone to stand in the gap to build a bridge and bring a message of hope and love to the people who are hurting. God is looking for you to stand up and say, "I am ready." I've said it before, and I'll say it again: You are God's special person, and He wants to use you for His work here on earth. You have an assignment you were created for, and that's to bring glory to God by helping as many people as you can.

> *"I looked for someone among them who would build up the wall and stand before me in the gap on behalf of the land so I would not have to destroy it, but I found no one."*
>
> **Ezekiel 22:30**

## Reflect

*Standing in the gap for God means standing in His place to accomplish His work here on earth. For you, that may look like sharing food with those who don't have any, or walking home with someone who is afraid to go by themselves, or even being that person who puts a smile on someone's face whenever they are down. Are you ready for that task? I know you are, and I can't wait to see you in action.*

## Respond

*Over the next seven days keep an eye out for people in your life who might be lonely or hurting. It could be a new kid at school who eats lunch alone, or your sibling who is going through a tough time. Think of ways you might be able to help them feel better.*

*Name:*

---

*Why I think they are hurting:*

---

*Ways I could help them feel better:*

---

*Name:*

---

*Why I think they are hurting:*

---

*Ways I could help them feel better:*

---

*Name:*

---

*Why I think they are hurting:*

---

*Ways I could help them feel better:*

---

Father, I take this responsibility to stand in the gap for your mission. Give me strength to do what you have called me to do. Amen.

WEEK 39

# DEVELOP AN ATTITUDE OF GRATITUDE

To show gratitude is to be positive about life and what it brings you. It's the quality of being thankful and willing to show appreciation and return the kindness whenever you can. Showing gratitude is deeper than just saying thank you—it's a mindset to carry everywhere you go.

King David always showed gratitude to God because He loved Him so much. The Bible says that David was a man after God's own heart, which means He loved God so much that He did everything to please Him. David carried this attitude of gratitude wherever he went, and throughout his life God was always with him. From the times David fought lions and bears as a shepherd boy to the day he defeated Goliath, God was always with him, even when he became King of Israel at 30 years old. God never left him, and that is most likely why David never gave up his attitude of gratitude. Throughout his 40 years as a king, he never lost a battle, but David understood that it wasn't due to his power or strength, but because God was always protecting him.

David made songs of thanksgiving praising God for how great and mighty He was. When you see how good God really is, you will be grateful for him at all times.

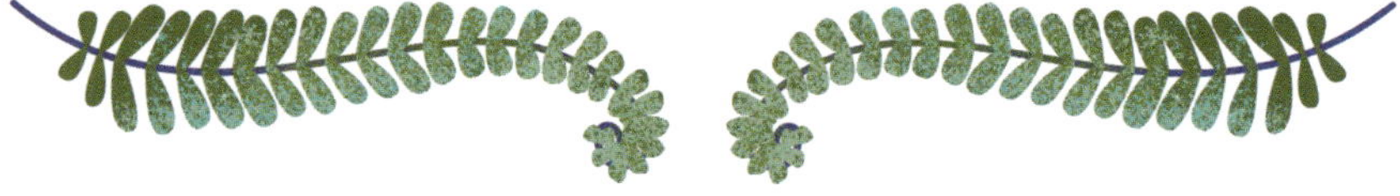

Did you know that gratitude is connected to happiness? The more gratitude have in your life, the happier you'll be. Here are a few examples of ways to show gratitude:

- Always say "thank you" when you receive something.
- Count your blessings. Think about how you woke up healthy this morning in your warm, cozy bed, or about the food you get to eat and the clothes you get to wear. These are blessings from God.
- Focus on the positive. Instead of focusing on the things you don't have, appreciate everything you do have, like a roof over your head. Instead of telling yourself that you're a failure, think about all the times you've succeeded and be grateful for those. Don't let negativity live in your mind or your heart.

*Give thanks to the Lord, for he is good;*
*his love endures forever.*

**Psalm 118:1**

## Reflect

*I get it—it's hard to be grateful when you're feeling unhappy, especially if you've had a bad day at school and you feel like nothing's going your way. But the trick is to make a small tweak in your mindset. Find one small thing to be grateful for—maybe it's the friend who always makes you laugh, or the fact that your favorite sports team won a game—and let that fill your heart.*

*Choose to be a person who will always show gratitude to God for what He has done in your life, so that you will be a living testimony of His greatness.*

CONTINUED ON NEXT PAGE ➡

CONTINUED FROM PREVIOUS PAGE

## Respond

*This week, as soon as you wake up each morning, write down one thing you're grateful for.*

*Before you go to sleep each night, write down something that happened that day that you're thankful for.*

*This will help you begin and end your days with an attitude of gratitude. And whenever you need to tweak your mindset toward happiness, you can revisit these lists.*

Thank you, Lord, for all you have done in my life. Help me always be thankful, help me always be positive, and help me always acknowledge the blessings you have put in my life. Amen.

# GOD LOOKS ON THE INSIDE

It's easy to judge someone on the way they look and dress. We might see people wearing expensive clothes and think they're rich and successful. Or maybe we automatically look down on someone whose clothes are dirty or shabby. A similar thing happened in the Bible when God wanted to choose a new King for Israel.

King Saul was a very tall, handsome man with broad shoulders who looked like the definition of a warrior. Though he was king for many years, he began disobeying God. So God decided to reject Saul as king and chose another young man, David, to take his place. When God told the prophet Samuel to find David in Jesse's house, Samuel started obsessing over whether the boy was tall enough to look like a king, since King Saul was very tall. But God told Samuel to stop worrying about David's appearance, because no matter how tall or short he was, he would still be king. What mattered was what was inside David's heart—that's what makes a great king.

This shows the importance of having a clean heart. A clean heart exists for God and wants to please God at all times. God doesn't look at what you wear or how you look; He cares about what's on the inside of you.

*But the Lord said to Samuel, "Do not look on his appearance or on the height of his stature, because I have rejected him. For the Lord sees not as man sees: man looks on the outward appearance, but the Lord looks on the heart."*

**1 Samuel 16:7 ESV**

## Reflect

*You can be neat and nicely put together with expensive clothes and still have a heart full of darkness. God wants you to be full of His light so it can shine bright for the world, no matter what you're wearing. So when you meet someone, focus on what's inside them.*

## Respond

*This week, take notice when you catch yourself judging someone based only on how they look. Each time, ask yourself these questions and note your answers here.*

*What judgment did I make about this person based on their appearance?*

---

*If I look inside their heart, what can I really learn about them?*

---

*What judgment did I make about this person based on their appearance?*

---

*If I look inside their heart, what can I really learn about them?*

---

CONTINUED ON NEXT PAGE ➡

CONTINUED FROM PREVIOUS PAGE

*What judgment did I make about this person based on their appearance?*

---

*If I look inside their heart, what can I really learn about them?*

---

Lord, cleanse my heart and make me pure so that you can use me for your glory like you used David. Help me have a heart full of light. Amen.

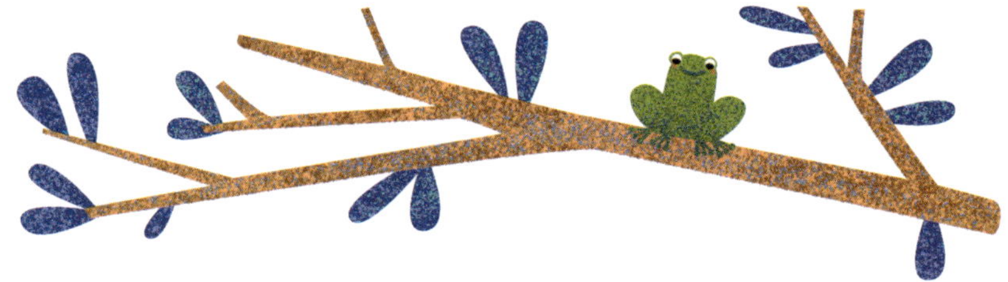

# GOD LOVES EVERYONE—AND SO SHOULD YOU!

Many terrible things are happening in the world right now that sometimes leave us speechless. In America, there has been a long fight about racism and equality. Racism is believing that a group of people are more important than others. But God is completely against this; the Bible says He shows no favoritism to anybody. He made us all and accepts us no matter where we're from or what the color of our skin is.

There was a time in the Bible when Peter was sitting with people who weren't Jewish, but when the Jewish people came, he got up and joined them. Paul got really angry at him and told Peter what he did was wrong because, as a child of God, he had to show love to everyone.

As children of God, we have to be willing to connect with people who may not be like us. That shows God's love in your heart. There's a reason none of us are the same. God made us unique because we are all special individuals with something different to offer to the world. For example, you might be good at writing, but your friend might be good at sports or music. And that means you can help each other out and learn new things.

*Then Peter began to speak: "I now realize how true it is that God does not show favoritism but accepts from every nation the one who fears him and does what is right."*

**Acts 10:34–35**

## Reflect

*Make this affirmation a part of your daily life: "I will love everyone the way God loves them. I will show kindness to everyone because it's the right thing to do. I will never show favoritism to specific people, but I will be fair to everyone. We are all God's children."*

## Respond

*Each morning this week, write down the name of someone in your school, church, or sports team who may be very different from you. Then think of a way you can try to connect with them.*

***Day 1***

*Name:*

---

*I can try to connect with them by:*

---

***Day 2***

*Name:*

---

*I can try to connect with them by:*

---

**Day 3**

*Name:*

*I can try to connect with them by:*

**Day 4**

*Name:*

*I can try to connect with them by:*

**Day 5**

*Name:*

*I can try to connect with them by:*

CONTINUED ON NEXT PAGE ➡

CONTINUED FROM PREVIOUS PAGE

**Day 6**

*Name:*

*I can try to connect with them by:*

**Day 7**

*Name:*

*I can try to connect with them by:*

Father, help me never show favoritism to anybody. Help me be fair, loving, and kind to all people at all times. Amen.

# LISTEN TO GOD WHEN HE SPEAKS

Have you ever heard of the guy who got swallowed by a whale? I know it sounds silly, but it's a true story. It happened in the Bible to a prophet named Jonah who was a preacher to the Israelites. One day, God asked Jonah to go and preach His word to the people in Nineveh because they were doing a lot of bad things at the time, and God wasn't pleased with them. Jonah was angry and didn't want to go because those people were one of the biggest enemies of the Israelites at the time. He didn't want them to be saved. He felt like they didn't deserve it.

Since Jonah made up his mind not to go, he boarded a boat and started sailing in the opposite direction to a place called Tarshish. When God saw what Jonah was doing, He sent a huge storm to surround the boat. The people on board blamed Jonah for making God angry, so they decided to throw him overboard. As soon as Jonah fell into the water, God sent a huge whale to swallow him so that he wouldn't drown and die. He still had a special mission to do. While Jonah was in the whale's stomach, he repented and praised God, asking Him for help.

After three days, God caused the whale to vomit Jonah out, and guess where he landed? On the shores of Nineveh. Jonah preached to the people of Nineveh and told them to repent, or God would destroy them in 40 days, and they would perish. The people heard and believed Jonah and repented. God showed them mercy and spared their lives because they turned away from their wickedness.

*Now the Lord provided a huge fish to swallow Jonah, and Jonah was in the belly of the fish three days and three nights.*

**Jonah 1:17**

## Reflect

*Often in our lives, God asks us to do things we might not want to do. Don't let your disobedience to God get you in a situation where He has to teach you a hard lesson.*

## Respond

*Spend time in prayer and write down three things God wants you to do this week. Check them off when you're done.*

- [ ] ____________________
- [ ] ____________________
- [ ] ____________________

Lord, help me be obedient to you and do what you ask me to do. I want to make you happy and fulfill my calling in life. Amen.

# THERE IS A TIME FOR EVERYTHING

Life comes with its seasons, and there is a time for everything. In the winter, it's freezing cold (especially where I live in Canada), and in the summer it's boiling hot. It shouldn't be hot in the winter because that's not its season, right? Another way to think about it is to imagine you see everyone crying because something very terrible just happened. That's not a time to start laughing, because it would be very insensitive and rude. There are times for sadness and times for laughter.

The book with this week's scripture is called Ecclesiastes. It's a very big word in the Old Testament that means "teacher" or "preacher." So the purpose was for the writer to get together all the wisdom he could and teach it to those who read the Bible. Wisdom means gathering all the information you can so that you can make good decisions with what you know. When we know God and have Him in our hearts all the time, it becomes easy for us to make wise decisions. This scripture teaches us that there is always a time for everything. Some days you are happy and some days you are sad. Some days are tough, while others are easy. This is the basic cycle of life, and it's important to understand.

But regardless of the things that happen in our lives, God is in control. He is with us every day, whether we go through good times or bad times. These feelings were created by God, and He wants us to use them and learn from them, but He doesn't want them to take over our lives. When something bad happens to somebody, they can think about it for a really long time and forget about the good things that have happened or continue to happen. But it's better to accept the situation, and then focus on the good things to come in the future. Live your life knowing that things will change consistently, but always put your trust in God.

> ***There is a time for everything, and a season for every activity under the heavens.***
>
> **Ecclesiastes 3:1**

## Reflect

*In life, you can't always control what happens, but you can control how you respond to it. How have you responded to situations in the past? With a positive or negative attitude? How could you shift your mindset to one of gratitude that focuses on the good things that have happened to you?*

*By taking more notice of your emotions, you can learn to shift your attitude. That doesn't mean that negative emotions aren't important—they are natural when something bad happens, and they help you know when something's wrong. But rather than dwelling on them for too long, it can help to think about the positive things the future might hold for you.*

## Respond

*At the end of each day this week, write down what made you feel sad, angry, or disappointed and why. Then think about how you can reframe the way you are feeling so that you can focus on the positive things in your life.*

***Day 1***

*Today I felt:*

*The reason I think I feel this way is:*

*One positive thing that happened today or that I am looking forward to is:*

## Day 2

*Today I felt:*

*The reason I think I feel this way is:*

*One positive thing that happened today or that I am looking forward to is:*

CONTINUED ON NEXT PAGE ➡

**Day 3**

*Today I felt:*

*The reason I think I feel this way is:*

*One positive thing that happened today or that I am looking forward to is:*

**Day 4**

*Today I felt:*

*The reason I think I feel this way is:*

*One positive thing that happened today or that I am looking forward to is:*

## Day 5

*Today I felt:*

*The reason I think I feel this way is:*

*One positive thing that happened today or that I am looking forward to is:*

## Day 6

*Today I felt:*

*The reason I think I feel this way is:*

*One positive thing that happened today or that I am looking forward to is:*

CONTINUED ON NEXT PAGE ➡

CONTINUED FROM PREVIOUS PAGE

**Day 7**

*Today I felt:*

*The reason I think I feel this way is:*

*One positive thing that happened today or that I am looking forward to is:*

God, help me accept the seasons of life I find myself in and respond to everything with a mind-set that "this is only for a certain amount of time." Thank you for your revelations and truths. Amen.

# GOD LOVES TO SHOW US MIRACLES!

God used a prophet by the name of Elijah to do some amazing things during his lifetime on earth. He told Elijah to leave his home and go to a gentile country called Zarephath, where there would be a widow who would take care of him when he got there. The thing I love about this story is that God performed two amazing miracles through Elijah while he was at the widow's house.

The first miracle happened when Elijah met the widow and asked her for food. She told him all she had left was a little bit of flour and oil because the entire country was suffering from drought and famine. They were so poor that they thought they wouldn't have enough food to make it to the next week. Elijah told the widow to still use what she had to make bread to feed him and the rest of her family. The flour and oil would last until God sent rain to the land so that the crops could grow. And it did! God sent Elijah to perform this miracle to show the people that if they put their trust in God, He would always provide for them, no matter how bad things seem.

The second miracle occurred when the widow's son got sick and stopped breathing. The mother was in such panic that she didn't know what to do. Her husband had already died, and now her son was dead too—that's a lot of pain to go through. But the story isn't over. Elijah came in and saw what had happened, and he cried out to God to raise her son. God listened to him and brought the boy back from death. When Elijah took the boy downstairs and showed the mother he was alive, everybody rejoiced and gave glory to God.

I know it may be hard to imagine these things happening now, but the Bible says that God is the same yesterday, today, and forever. So if God is still the same God, He is still a miracle-working God, and you can trust Him to perform a miracle in your life.

> *Then he stretched himself out on the boy three times and cried out to the Lord, "Lord my God, let this boy's life return to him!" The Lord heard Elijah's cry, and the boy's life returned to him, and he lived.*
>
> **1 Kings 17:21–22**

## Reflect

*God is still in the business of creating miracles in our lives. Many things happen that we cannot fix on our own, and we need God to perform a miracle for us. Just as Elijah cried out to God for help, you can do the same thing.*

## Respond

*The faith it takes to move mountains is the same faith you need for God to create a miracle. We all need God to do something amazing for us or someone we know. And He probably has already performed some miracles for you! This week, think back on your life and any miracles that may have happened thanks to God, and note them here.*

*Now, I want you to write down one miracle you trust that God will perform for you. You can return to this page and check it off when God answers.*

You are the God of miracles. The all-powerful one. Lord, help me see the miracles you're creating in our lives every day and build my faith to truly believe in what you say you will do. Amen.

# WORSHIP THE ONE TRUE GOD, NOT A GOLDEN COW

The story of Moses going up the mountain to get the Ten Commandments from God is a very interesting one. God called Moses to go up Mount Sinai and stay there for 40 days and 40 nights, receiving instructions on the tabernacle and offering. God gave him two stone tablets that had the Ten Commandments written on them by the finger of God.

While Moses was on the mountain, the Israelites thought he had been there for too long and started wondering what was happening. They became impatient with Moses and began begging a priest named Aaron to make them an idol they could worship as their god instead. Aaron told the Israelites to take off all their gold earrings and give them to him so that he could make an idol out of the gold. He melted them down and formed a golden calf, telling them, "Israel, this is your god who brought you out of Egypt." The people held a festival worshiping and praising the golden calf. This was considered a sin because God commanded them that they should have no other gods before Him.

When Moses saw what the Israelites were doing, he became furious, and he smashed the two tablets on the ground and broke the commandments. The anger in him was burning because he saw that God's children had fallen back into sin. While he was still angry, he took the golden calf that Aaron had made, burned it up, and ground it into powder. He scattered the powder on a lake and made the Israelites drink that water.

If I were Moses, I'd be really angry too. He had just had a conversation with the one true God, and now the Israelites were worshiping something made of material things instead of worshiping God. Imagine praying to a god who can't see you, hear you, or help you. That's what the Israelites were doing with the golden calf. God hates idol worship because it means you're putting a material item before Him. There's only one true God who can help you and hear you when you call Him.

> ***Aaron answered them, "Take off the gold earrings that your wives, your sons and your daughters are wearing, and bring them to me." So all the people took off their earrings and brought them to Aaron.***
>
> **Exodus 32:2–3**

## Reflect

*Are there things in your life that you might be putting before God? Like your video games, TV shows, or sports? These things aren't bad, but they become idolatry when you start putting them first over everything else that's important, especially God. If you decide to skip your prayers because you've been up late watching TV and you're too tired, that's an example of putting something before God. Or maybe you always choose to read comic books instead of the Bible. That doesn't mean you can't read comic books, but just make sure it doesn't take away from the time you could be spending with God.*

CONTINUED ON NEXT PAGE ➡

CONTINUED FROM PREVIOUS PAGE

## Respond

*Write a list of things you do more often than you read the Bible, pray, or spend time with God.*

*Figure out if these things have become idols in your life. This week, change your routine and start putting the important things first.*

God, I'm sorry if I have ever put anything before you. I promise to make you first in my life and put nothing before you. Amen.

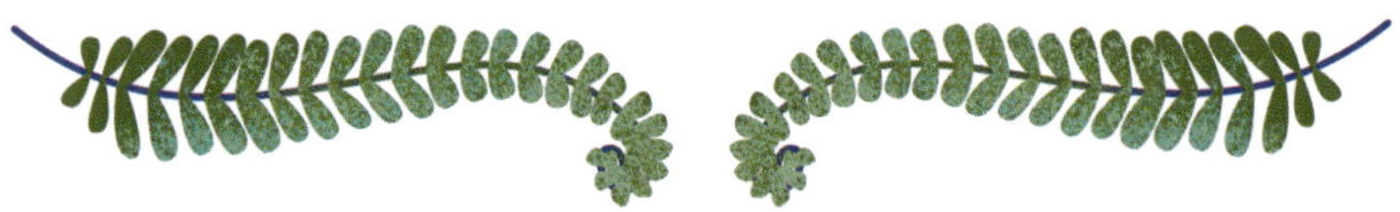

# SHINE LIKE PURE GOLD!

There was a guy in the Bible named Job, who was a rich and righteous man. God loved Job very much and was pleased with the life that he was living because he always obeyed God. One day, Satan was roaming across the earth when he saw God and started having a conversation with him. God asked Satan if he had noticed His servant, Job, saying about him, "No one on this earth is like him—a man of perfect integrity who fears God and turns away from evil."

When I read this, I was extremely impressed with Job and even had a desire to be like him. How awesome would it be for God to say these things about you? But there's more to the story. Satan started saying that Job is only like that because God had already given him everything, and he always had God's protection. God and Satan then came to an agreement that He would allow Satan to do anything he wanted to everything and everyone around Job to test him, but that he couldn't kill him.

So after this agreement, the first thing Satan tried to mess with were Job's children, then his servants, then his animals, and lastly his crops. Satan tried to harm everything he thought would make Job turn away from God. But then Job said something very powerful. He said that he came to this world with nothing, and he would take nothing with him when he left. So he was not obeying God because of the stuff that he had; he was obeying God because he loved Him and wanted to honor Him. The whole purpose of this situation wasn't to ruin Job's life and make him miserable, but to sanctify Job and purify him to make him even better. That's why God gave Satan a restriction on what he could do. God is the most powerful person, and nothing happens without Him knowing and approving.

After Job proved his integrity to all those around him, God then gave him double of everything that he had. So even though everything looked bad at one point, it was just to prepare him for the best things that were to come. In 1 Peter 1:7, it talks about how gold has to be tested by fire to see its genuineness, and it's the same thing for Christians. Sometimes God allows you to go through some tough things to purify you, so you come out and shine like pure gold. When you're tested by fire, it shows who you truly are and how tough you are. This is a good thing, so don't be afraid.

> *But he knows the way that I take; when he has tested me, I will come forth as gold.*
>
> **Job 23:10**

## Reflect

*When you go through something hard, does it sometimes feel like God isn't there with you? Well, He's always with you, and He's there to help you get through whatever you're up against. God's greatest desire is for you to become all that He created you to be.*

## Respond

*This week, find some older Christians in your life—at your dinner table, at your church, or maybe your teachers at school—and talk to them about the hard times they've been through. Here are some questions to ask:*

*What has been one of your greatest challenges?*
*What lesson did you learn from it?*
*How did it strengthen your faith in God?*

*At the end of the week, write down what you've learned from those people about faith.*

Lord, thank you for always working on our hearts and making us into your image. Help us understand that you're not punishing us but purifying us. Amen.

# GODLY MUSIC BRINGS HEALING

I've had a love and passion for music since I was in the third grade. I knew that someday I would start making music, but I was just scared to try. Eventually, when I went to high school, there was an older man who had a music label, and he signed me as his youngest artist. I started officially recording music in the ninth grade, and from there I never turned back. I still make music today, and it's my mission as a Christian to make music that is uplifting and positive, that people can listen to and use to grow closer to God. As the years have gone by, I've received many random messages from people telling me that my music changed their life, or impacted them in a positive way. Music is really that powerful.

There's a story in the Bible about David playing the harp for King Saul, who had an evil spirit tormenting him. This spirit would always come and bother Saul, and he just wanted it to leave him alone and never come back. David, the son of Jesse, was great at playing the harp. He was also a brave warrior who could speak well, and was known to always have the Lord with him. Jesse sent David with a donkey and a goat and told him to go to King Saul to serve him. Any time the spirit would come and torment Saul, David would play the harp for him to relax his soul, and the spirit would leave.

Music is such a powerful tool and that's why we use it for praise and worship. We listen to it in the car, at home, at church—everywhere. But it's important to understand that music affects our moods and emotions in both good and bad ways. Remember how the Bible tells us to be mindful of the things we watch and listen to? There is music that can hurt you, and there is music that can heal you. So make sure to listen to the things that will build you up and not tear you down. Listen to words of encouragement.

> *Whenever the spirit from God came on Saul, David would take up his lyre and play. Then relief would come to Saul; he would feel better, and the evil spirit would leave him.*
>
> **1 Samuel 16:23**

## Reflect

*What types of music do you listen to on a regular basis? Do you listen to songs that are uplifting and powerful, or do you listen to the songs everybody else listens to on the radio because it's cool? Those popular songs often contain language and themes that aren't good for you and can potentially fill you with negative emotions.*

## Respond

*Search YouTube, Spotify, or Apple Music for uplifting artists whose music helps you in your faith. If you like their message, but don't like the sound, keep searching for another artist where you may like both. There are so many wonderful Christian artists out there that you'll definitely find some you like. Each day this week, add a new song to your playlist and note why that song is uplifting to your faith.*

CONTINUED ON NEXT PAGE ➡

CONTINUED FROM PREVIOUS PAGE

**Day 1**

*Song/Artist:*

---

*What I find uplifting about this music:*

---

---

**Day 2**

*Song/Artist:*

---

*What I find uplifting about this music:*

---

---

**Day 3**

*Song/Artist:*

---

*What I find uplifting about this music:*

---

---

**Day 4**

*Song/Artist:*

*What I find uplifting about this music:*

**Day 5**

*Song/Artist:*

*What I find uplifting about this music:*

**Day 6**

*Song/Artist:*

*What I find uplifting about this music:*

CONTINUED ON NEXT PAGE ➡

CONTINUED FROM PREVIOUS PAGE

**Day 7**

*Song/Artist:*

---

*What I find uplifting about this music:*

---

---

Heavenly Father, thank you for the gift of music. I understand that music is everywhere we go. Therefore I pray that the music and the things that I listen to are uplifting and glorifying to your name. Amen.

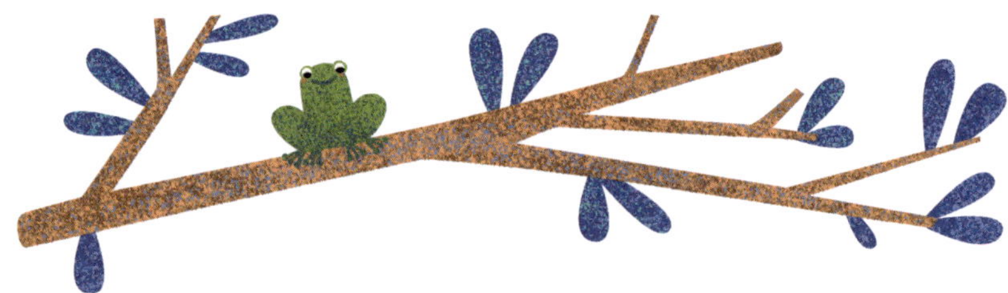

# WHAT ARE YOUR PRIORITIES?

As you continue to grow and slowly transition into your teenage years, your life will get busier. Instead of focusing on one thing, you're going to have to focus on three or four things at the same time. In high school, you don't just stay in one class; you have multiple subjects that you have to do in a day. And if you participate in extracurricular activities, such as sports or clubs, you'll have even more on your plate. When things start to get hard in life, you can't just drop everything and quit—you have to find a way to make it work so you can accomplish your goals. This means working out what your priorities are.

So let's say, for example, that you have a project to work on that's due on Friday, and it's Wednesday. But then your best friend asks you to play some video games—what do you think the best thing to do is? I think it's best to finish your project first so that you don't have to think about it anymore once it's done. When you've finished it, your mind will be clear of any assignments that you have to complete, and you can just enjoy playing video games. Plus it means you'll do a better job on your project because you won't be rushing it. This is how priorities work—choose the most important things to get done first and then do the things you want to do after.

How about if you have some chores to do, like cleaning your room, but your little brother comes to you and says, "Let's go shoot some hoops." It might be tempting to leave your chores for another day and go straight to playing basketball. But that's not taking the responsibility that earns you independence and freedom like we talked about earlier in this book. By doing your chores first, you'll not only have more free time for yourself, but you won't have to worry about getting in trouble. I know chores aren't the most fun things to do, but when you get your priorities right, everything becomes easier.

Jesus told Christians to get their priorities right by seeking the kingdom of God first before anything. And if you do that, He'll make sure you get everything you need. A lot of us focus on things that aren't as important as God, and we start to forget where we want to go. But God says that if you follow Him and make Him a priority, He will always be with you and help you in your times of need.

> *But seek first his kingdom and his righteousness, and all these things will be given to you as well.*
>
> **Matthew 6:33**

## Reflect

*What things take priority in your life? Are you just focused on having fun with your friends and only doing things you enjoy? Or do you accept your responsibilities and make sure you prioritize being a good, reliable person who always does what they are asked to do without complaining? God wants you to take care of the important things first, and then go on to other things.*

## Respond

*Write a list of chores and the things that you have to do. Also write a list of things you enjoy doing. This week, focus on how you can balance these two lists, prioritizing the important things first but allowing yourself to still enjoy fun things as a reward.*

| IMPORTANT THINGS | FUN THINGS |
|---|---|
| | |
| | |
| | |
| | |
| | |

Thank you, heavenly Father, for letting me see the important things. Help me focus on you first and everything else after. Amen.

# SPEND MORE TIME WITH GOD

How early do you wake up every morning? Did you know Jesus woke up around two or three a.m. every single morning just to pray? He made God a priority every day so that he could remain close with Him. God was the most important thing to Jesus, so he made spending time with Him a major thing in his life. How do you usually feel in the morning? Tired? Jesus was probably tired too, but no matter how he felt, he got himself out of bed early to pray before his busy day began.

In this Christian life, sacrifice is something that you have to get used to doing. It might not be sleep you have to sacrifice, but that word is something that will show up often in your life if you really want to be serious about your relationship with God. This is a very important topic because Jesus sacrificed everything that he had to save you because he loves you. He was the creator of this world. He had all the riches in heaven as he was a king with a kingdom. And he was able to heal and create miracles because he had the power of God inside him. In fact, he was so powerful that he rose up from the grave. Who wouldn't want to spend more time with someone like this? He's amazing. The best thing about your relationship with God is that the more you spend time with Him, the more you start becoming like Him. You think like Him, you act like Him, and you speak His words more clearly.

Jesus made it a daily practice to spend time with God, not only for those reasons, but also to give him strength for the day and in all that he did. Even though Jesus was much more powerful than any of you, he still prayed for strength every day. So if your savior was doing that, it's something you must do. Find time to spend with God every day—you don't always have to do it in the morning, but instead you can do it in the afternoon or right before you go to sleep. Once you get into the habit of doing it, it will become second nature to you, and you may even find yourself wanting to dedicate more time to spending with God.

> ***Very early in the morning, while it was still dark, Jesus got up, left the house and went off to a solitary place, where he prayed.***
>
> **Mark 1:35**

## Reflect

*What's your daily routine? How much time do you spend with God? Sacrifice is a major thing in the walk of faith, and sometimes you might have to give up time for things you really love for God.*

## Respond

*Look at your schedule for this week and see where you can set aside some time to spend with God each day. You might need to give something up, like watching a TV show or reading a comic book, but the sacrifice will be worth it. Make sure you spend time with God every single day this week.*

CONTINUED ON NEXT PAGE ➡

CONTINUED FROM PREVIOUS PAGE

*At the end of the week, write about how it made you feel to prioritize being in God's company.*

Lord, help me spend even more time with you. Strengthen me on this walk of faith and help me grow into your image and likeness. Amen.

# GOD DOESN'T BRING TEMPTATION

God is love, God is king, and God is righteous. But sometimes people try to ruin the image of God and make Him look different from what He really is so that we won't believe in Him. When that happens, it's important to remember that God would never put us in a position that makes us do anything against His word. That's just Satan trying to tempt us. He steals everything that God gives to you, he tries to kill your joy and passion for God, and tries to destroy all the plans that God has for you. But because you're a child of God, the devil can never win. God has got your back.

So when you face times of temptation, understand that it is not God who is doing it to you; it's the evil one who is trying to confuse you so that you go on the wrong path. Follow God's path and God's way, and you will never lose in this life. I told you in the beginning that I'm your coach. It's my job to lead you to victory, and there is only victory in God. So don't fall for the trap of the evil one—use the power of God to overcome every temptation that comes your way, and live a life of victory, inspiring others to walk down the same path.

***When tempted, no one should say, "God is tempting me." For God cannot be tempted by evil, nor does he tempt anyone.***

**James 1:13**

## Reflect

*Have you felt that you have been tempted lately with certain things? To lie, cheat, or steal? You're human, so you might have these feelings once in a while. But remember that they're not from God, so when those thoughts come, fight them with prayer.*

## Respond

*Throughout this week, notice when you are being led into temptation, and write those things down here so that you can pray about each topic. God loves when we are specific in our prayers because it gives Him a specific topic to work on. Don't be afraid to tell Him the truth. He is always willing to forgive you.*

Father, thank you for letting us see the devil's tricks. Because of you we have the power to overcome any plan that He has for us. You are an amazing God. Amen.

# COUNT YOUR BLESSINGS

God has done so much for you that if you were to sit and count all your blessings, it would be nearly impossible to get them all. Imagine counting all the stars in the sky. That's literally how many blessings God gives us regularly. Some people don't know what I mean by that. But let's look at this for a second: Did you wake up this morning? Do you have clothes and shoes to wear to school or outside? Do you have a bed to sleep on? A place to take a shower? Food to eat? And a place you can call home?

If you said yes to a majority of those things, you are blessed beyond measure. Remember how we figured out a few weeks ago that more than half of the world lives off five dollars or less a day? Well, all the things I've just mentioned can be added up to much more than that. God loves you and put you here for a reason, and you are blessed in that way so you can be a blessing to others, not to just keep everything for yourself. When things aren't going your way or you don't get something that you really wanted, think about people all around the world who have absolutely nothing. Think about the boys your age who didn't eat today, and the people who will never have what you have. Count your blessings and name them one by one, because God has done so much for you, and He deserves all the glory for that.

*The Lord bless you and keep you; the Lord make his face shine on you and be gracious to you; the Lord turn his face toward you and give you peace.*

**Numbers 6:24–26**

## Reflect

*How many blessings do you think you have? Try to estimate a number. Do you think there might be more blessings coming? God is an awesome God.*

## Respond

*Each day this week, list a blessing from God and share it with a friend or family member. Explain why it was such a blessing to you and how you can potentially share it with others. Whenever you need a reminder of how blessed you are, you can return to read over this list.*

1. ______________________
2. ______________________
3. ______________________
4. ______________________
5. ______________________
6. ______________________
7. ______________________

> Your blessings, O Lord, are too much for me to count. I want to thank you for always thinking of me and loving me the way that you do. Amen.

# I AM A SPOKESPERSON FOR THE KINGDOM!

The gospel is so precious and so pure. It's our only ticket to heaven. Imagine if you were in a burning building—wouldn't you wake up everyone else and tell them that there's a fire, and they need to get out? It's the same thing with the gospel. There's a place that many people are headed to, and it's not heaven, so they need someone to save them. There is only one person they can go to and be saved, but many people don't truly know this person. They've heard of His name, and they've heard of what He's done, but they haven't truly accepted it for themselves. If they don't accept the truth about it, then it means nothing to them.

Sometimes people just don't understand because they didn't have anybody to teach them about it. And this is where the evangelist comes in. An evangelist is someone who is a spokesperson for the kingdom and shares the gospel with as many people as possible. They can then take those people to heaven with them to live forever with God. Without the evangelist, so many people would never hear about the name Jesus and the saving power he has.

Paul encouraged Timothy to do the work of an evangelist, which is to continually preach Jesus to the world, and today I want to give you that same assignment. Go out into the world and preach the gospel so people can be saved. God has called you as a spokesperson for His kingdom—someone to speak about, preach, and defend the gospel. Though God is the ultimate hero, you will play a huge part in the story of saving the world! Don't you want to save the world?

> ***But you, keep your head in all situations, endure hardship, do the work of an evangelist, discharge all the duties of your ministry.***
>
> **2 Timothy 4:5**

## Reflect

*Devote yourself to being a mouthpiece for God and doing the work of an evangelist to save the world from temptation and harm!*

## Respond

*Write down the simple steps I've taught you in this book about how you can receive Jesus.*

*Work each day this week to memorize them so you can share them anywhere, at any time.*

Thank you, God, for your gospel. Thank you, Lord, for saving me and making me your own. Help me not fear when I am preaching your word. Help me be as bold as a lion and bring people to your kingdom. Amen.

# ABOUT THE AUTHOR

**Lord Badu** is a husband, father, author, artist, and coach whose goal is to make the whole counsel of God clear and applicable to our everyday lives. He wants to inspire people to be all that God has created them to be, and create practical guidelines to help them get there. His desire is to coach people by edifying, elevating, and inspiring them in Godliness first, and then in every other area of their lives. Lord is married to his amazing wife and has two young children, Eden and Lord Jr. Aside from writing books, recording music, and public speaking, he is a basketball enthusiast and loves to keep active and stay competitive.